HOW TO READ GENESIS

TREMPER LONGMAN III

IVP Academic

An imprint of InterVarsity Press
Downers Grove, Illinois

InterVarsity Press
P.O. Box 1400, Downers Grove, IL 60515-1426
World Wide Web: www.ivpress.com
E-mail: email@ivpress.com

Paternoster Press
An imprint of Authentic Media
9 Holdom Avenue, Bletchley, Milton Keynes MK1 1QR, England
World Wide Web: www.authenticmedia.co.uk/paternoster

Design: Kathleen Lay Burrows
Images: Roberta Polfus

USA ISBN 978-0-87784-943-8
UK ISBN 978-1-84227-385-2

Printed in the United States of America ∞

Library of Congress Cataloging-in-Publication Data

Longman, Tremper.
  How to read Genesis / Tremper Longman.
    p. cm.
  Includes bibliographical references and indexes.
  ISBN 0-87784-943-9 (pbk.: alk. paper)
  1. Bible. O.T. Genesis—Criticism, interpretation, etc. I. Title.
  BS1235.52.L67 2005
  222'.1107—dc22

                                                                                                                                2005001666

P 21 20 19 18 17 16 15 14 13 12 11 10 9 8 7 6

Y 24 23 22 21 20 19 18 17 16 15 14 13 12 11

Dedicated to ministers of the gospel.

In particular

Julian Alexander

Fran Park

Bruce Erickson

Jim Petty

David Clowney

Ron Jenkins

Neil Tolsma

Lawrence Eyres

Dick Gerber

Jack Miller

Ron Lutz

John Yenchko

Roy Clements

Harold Bussell

Meiji Working

Al Silvera

Tim Keller

CONTENTS

Acknowledgments 9

Preface 13

PART I: READING GENESIS WITH A STRATEGY 17

1   Understanding the Book of "Beginnings" 19

PART II: READING GENESIS AS LITERATURE 41

2   Who Wrote Genesis? 43

3   The Shape of the Book of Genesis 59

PART III: READING GENESIS IN ITS OWN WORLD 69

4   Myth or History? Genesis and the *Enuma Elish* 71

5   Noah and Utnapishtim:
    Whose Flood Story Should We Trust? 81

6   Abraham and Nuzi:
    Patriarchal Customs in Their Cultural Context 88

PART IV: READING GENESIS AS GOD'S STORY 99

7   The Primeval History: Genesis 1—11 101

8   The Patriarchal Narratives: Genesis 12—36 126

9   The Joseph Story: Genesis 37—50 149

PART V: READING GENESIS AS CHRISTIANS 163

10   The Christological Difference 165

Appendix: Commentaries on the Book of Genesis 177

Notes 181

Names Index 188

Subject Index 189

Scripture Index 190

ACKNOWLEDGMENTS

Writing a book on biblical interpretation is both a great privilege and a great responsibility. Writing a book on the proper interpretation of a book like Genesis intensifies both.

The responsibility comes with the importance of the subject matter. The Bible is the Word of God and Genesis is the foundation stone of that great literary edifice. In Genesis we learn of God's creation, human rebellion and God's pursuit to redeem us. In Genesis we meet Adam and Eve, Noah, Abraham, Joseph, and many other compelling persons. Genesis begins with the creation and ends with Israel in Egypt, encompassing an unknown but certainly vast length of time. In Genesis, as I hope to establish in the following pages, we get the first intimations of our Redeemer.

The responsibility also results from the controversies associated with this book. Opinions run hot about the nature of the creation, the historicity of the material, its anticipation of future events, not to speak of its date and authorship. To people of faith and many others, these are important matters.

Of course the privilege is made of the same stuff as the responsibilities. It is a privilege to be able to encourage the reader's thinking about important interpretive issues surrounding this monumental book. And, indeed, though it will be manifestly clear that I have arrived at a number of hermeneutical and exegetical conclusions, my main desire is to stimulate readers into thinking through these issues for themselves.

I didn't start with a desire to write on Genesis. I had already written books in what has turned into a short series on Psalms and Proverbs,[1] and encouraged by their reception, I approached InterVarsity Press about writing a third book. I made some suggestions as to which book I would tackle, and Dan Reid pushed me toward Genesis because of its popularity.

It did not take much convincing; I welcomed the opportunity to spend more time with that book, but I soon realized just how difficult it would be to write on Genesis. As a monumental and controversial book, I knew I could not cover everything and certainly could never satisfy everyone. My guess is that there is something here that may irritate or even anger everyone who has an opinion already formed on Genesis. My hope is that people will be open to question their previous opinions as they engage the book again. I have tried to do the same as I wrote this book, and I found that I did change my mind on some issues. When it comes to biblical interpretation, the foundational things are crystal clear, but many other matters are debatable.

I would like to acknowledge those who have significantly helped me, while relieving them of responsibility concerning final conclusions. Their reading of my manuscript gave me much to think about, and I often, but not always, accepted their criticism and advice. I would like to thank John Walton and the other (anonymous) reader of my manuscript. They were both intended to be blind referees but John rightly knew that I would know who he was by the nature of his advice since we have been friends and occasional sparring partners on some hermeneutical issues for years. I learned and revised many things because of John's input. I also learned much from the other reviewer. On matters concerning chapter ten, I received conflicting advice (John was hesitant and the other reader wanted me to expand), so there I felt free to keep things as they were!

But the one who deserves the most praise for encouraging and guiding this project is my main editor at InterVarsity Press, Dan Reid. Dan is a first-rate biblical scholar and editor. We have written a book together (*God Is a Warrior* [Zondervan, 1995]), and this is the third book of mine that he has edited. Furthermore, I have worked with him as an editor on one published book (*Dictionary of Biblical Imagery*), and we are presently working on another. He is meticulous, encouraging, energetic, intelligent and fun to be around. (I am not just saying this because I would like to work with him in the future!)

However, since it is a little dubious to dedicate a book to your editor, I have chosen instead to dedicate this book to ministers who have had a large influence on my thinking and life. I do this as a token of my great respect and love for those in ministry. As a former teacher at a seminary, I know how tough it can be to be a minister. These men and women have made significant sacrifice to be our spiritual guides. The ones I name are not all those I should, and the ones I name are not necessarily ones that I would agree with on Genesis today, but they nurtured me at various important times in my life, and for that I am grateful. My hope is that this book will help them and other ministers continue to enrich their own lives and the lives of their congregations in the Word of God.

Tremper Longman III

Beginnings. We can learn a great deal about people if we know their origins. People often want to know their roots in order to come to a better understanding of themselves. Such interest motivates the study of national history as well as our own personal genealogy.

But there is something even more important, more fundamental, than our family past or our national or ethnic origins. What about the beginning of the human race? Who are we? Were we made with a purpose? Does our existence have meaning beyond our mere lifetimes? These are some of the fundamental questions that nag us as we reflect on life.

But there are even more questions. What is our relationship with the rest of creation? Is it there for our use, or are we simply one of a large variety of animals that prowl the earth, none more privileged than another? Was the world created for us, or are we simply an accident of chemical and biological processes?

Even more basic, is there anything that is beyond the physical? Is what we see all there is, or is there something spiritual that cannot be detected directly by the senses? And most important: what about God? Is there a God, and if so, what is he like and how do we relate to him?

These questions about origins are foundational questions, and the book of Genesis, though not answering all our foundational questions, addresses many of them.

Early tradition recognized this when it gave Genesis its name. In Hebrew tradition the book was known by its first phrase, *bereshit,* "in the beginning." The English title "Genesis" comes from the Greek word that means "origins," since it was recognized that this book provided a description of the origins of the universe, the earth, animate life in general as well as human beings. Furthermore, the book narrates the origins of Israel, the people through whom God chose to bring his blessing to the world.

The book of Genesis, concerned with origins, is very much a foundational book. It is the foundation of the Torah (also known as the Pentateuch), the Old Testament and ultimately the entire Christian Bible. We will fully explore the foundational quality of Genesis throughout this study, but here I will provide a few words of introductory comment.

We often think of Genesis as an isolated book within the canon, the first of the Hebrew Bible. It describes the period from the beginning of time, through the patriarchal period, to the severe famine that drove the family of God to Egypt. The next book, Exodus, begins several centuries after the close of Genesis. Exodus is tightly connected to the rest of the Torah, since the books of the Torah are all concerned with Israel's journey through the wilderness.

The book of Genesis is not properly understood unless it is seen as the first chapter of a five-chapter work we refer to as the Torah, or the Pentateuch. While it may have been written using earlier sources, it was not written at the time of the events it describes, but rather, at the earliest, in the period after the exodus, and it was written very much as a prehistory providing the base of the story of exodus and wilderness wandering that follows.

Second, and this will be harder to see until we deal with the life of Abraham, the book of Genesis is the foundation for the rest of the Old Testament as well as the whole Bible, including the New Testament. When we read through the book of Genesis, we see that its ending anticipates that more is to come. The last major character, Joseph, dies, but he gives instructions that he is to be buried not in the land of Egypt but in the land that God has promised to give to the descendants of Abraham. When the Torah ends, the descendants of Abraham are poised on the border of the Promised Land, about to go in. We cannot understand the history of redemption of the people of Israel from beginning to end without the book of Genesis. The same is true of the good news concerning Jesus Christ (of which a full explanation will come later). Already in the book of Genesis, Christ's redemptive work is anticipated, and without this foundational book we cannot understand the significance of Jesus' death and resurrection.

Last, we should see a special connection between the very beginning of the Bible and its end. Genesis 1—2 narrates the creation of the cosmos and humanity. God places Adam and Eve in the Garden that contains the tree of life. Genesis 3 narrates the fracture of that relationship, and from that point through Revelation 20 we hear the story of redemption, how God pursued humans to restore his blessing on then. It is of great significance that the last two chapters of Revelation (Rev 21—22) use language reminiscent of the Garden of Eden to describe the time of final reunion with God. The end brings us back to the beginning.

The Bible is made up of many different books, but it is also a single book, of which the book of Genesis is the first chapter. As such it initiates the plot of the whole. In chapter seven and following I will argue that the theme of Genesis centers around the idea of God's blessing on his human creatures. Genesis 1—2 describes a situation in which Adam and Eve are given abundant life. In particular, we should note Genesis 1:28: "Then God blessed them and said, 'Be fruitful and multiply. Fill the earth and govern it.'" Here we see God's blessing connected both to descendants and land, an association that will reverberate in the rest of the book and beyond.[2] However, the plot is complicated by the fact that Adam and Eve rebel against God in Genesis 3. The rest of the book shows God's relentless pursuit to restore the relationship. Indeed, again, this is the theme of the rest of the Bible that only comes to conclusion in its final two chapters and the description of the New Jerusalem, a metaphor for heaven, where human beings will again, as in the Garden, live in the very presence of God.

Why read the book of Genesis? To understand our origins. To understand who we are, our meaning in life. To comprehend our place in the world, our relationship with other creatures, with other humans and with God himself. To recognize the significance of the rest of redemptive history culminating in the ministry of Jesus Christ.

In other words, it is difficult to overstate the importance of Genesis to our lives today. However, as numerous controversies concerning its interpretation well illustrate, Genesis is not always easy to understand. The purpose of *How to Read Genesis* is to explore the interpretation of the book of Genesis. In the process I will present an overarching understanding of the book itself, but in addition, I want to reflect on the principles of interpretation that are most important to arriving at a proper understanding of the book. It is to these principles that we turn in the next chapter.

READING GENESIS
WITH A STRATEGY

■ ■ ■

This book is not a commentary, though it will provide an overarching interpretation of Genesis, especially in chapters 7-9. Like its predecessors in this series, which examine Psalms and Proverbs,[1] *How to Read Genesis* is an exploration of the proper interpretive approach to the book of Genesis. Since many of us have grown up hearing the stories of Genesis (creation, fall, flood), they sound so familiar. However, we need to be reminded that they were written in an ancient context. Perhaps the interpretations we grew up with are correct, but on further study they may need to be adjusted.

The truth of the matter is that the proper interpretation of any piece of literature, and in particular a text as ancient and as important as the Bible, deserves our careful reflection. Chapter one will provide the interpretive tools to improve our understanding of Genesis. As we do so, we will observe that Genesis is a different type of book than Psalms or Proverbs, and thus we will have to fine-tune our interpretive strategy.

The strategy will focus on discovering the intention of the human author. Otherwise, we run the risk of importing all kinds of foreign ideas into the ancient text. However, we must never forget that Genesis is part of the canon and thus claims ultimate divine authority. God used human authors to produce the Bible, but he is the ultimate author. While we ground our interpretation in what we propose is the meaning of the human author, we also believe that the divine intention can transcend that of the human author. However, we can only recognize this if a later author brings this meaning out. This will be the subject of chapter ten.

You might get the impression from what follows that interpretation is simply a matter of the intellect, involving research and analytical thinking. While there is too much unreflective Bible reading among Christians, interpretation is not a mere intellectual exercise. It is a spiritual discipline. After all, for those who believe that God is the ultimate author of the Bible, the message of 1 Corinthians 2:14 is relevant: "only those who are spiritual can understand what the Spirit means." We read the Bible to hear the words of God. In order to keep this from becoming a one-way conversation, Bible study should be accompanied by prayer, asking God to open our eyes to its truth. After all, truth involves more than intellectual statements; it includes acting on what we believe, making the Bible's teaching a part of our lives. Many Christians need to hear this message.

Chapter one presents the important principles of interpretation by means of questions to ask the text. (A summary of these questions may be found at the end of the chapter.)

UNDERSTANDING THE
BOOK OF "BEGINNINGS"

Genesis is not an easy book to understand. It takes hard work to come to grips with this ancient, enigmatic book. To really get under the surface of Genesis we can benefit from the work of professionals, those whom God has called to devote their careers to the study of the Scriptures.

As I make this statement, I anticipate resistance on the part of some readers. "No," they might protest, "God speaks to us clearly in his Word. All we have to do is pick it up and read it. We don't need to spend a long time thinking about principles of interpretation. The work of scholars obscures rather than clarifies the simple, literal meaning of the Bible."

I support much of the sentiment expressed in this hypothetical reaction. Even if they are not really aware of it, the protest is based on the important doctrines of the priesthood of all believers and the perspicuity and sufficiency of Scripture.

The priesthood of all believers (based most explicitly on passages like Jer 31:33-35 and 1 Pet 2:9) tells us that we can all have a personal and intimate relationship with God without some kind of human intermediary. The Reformers, people like Luther and Calvin, asserted this truth over against traditional church doctrine that insisted on the necessity of professional clerics. Such a viewpoint also helps explain why for many years the Roman Catholic Church resisted translation of the Bible into people's everyday language and kept it in Latin, which only the priests could read and understand. In the Catholic Church a layperson's relationship with the Bible only changed in the 1960s at Vatican Council II. So it may be in defense of the important idea of the priesthood of all believers that some readers will be skeptical about my urging the help of professional interpreters.

The Reformers argued strongly for the clarity (perspicuity) of Scripture. They rightly held that the Bible was not written in a code. Further, they defended the view that the Bible could be understood on its own terms (sufficiency of Scripture). We do not need the tradition of the church fathers to understand the Bible.

When rightly understood, these doctrines are fundamentally important and crucial to defend. The problem is that the priesthood of all believers as well as the perspicuity and sufficiency of Scripture have been wrongly understood and applied in areas they were never intended to be applied. In short, what the Reformers understood the Bible to teach was that the message of salvation in the Bible is clear and understandable to all without the need of a priestly mediator or scholarly input. That human beings are sinners in need of a Savior and that the Savior is none other than Jesus Christ is patently clear in Scripture.

However, not everything is equally plain. How long is the "day" of Genesis 1? Was the flood universal? Who are the Nephilim? Why do some verses say that the Ishmaelites took Joseph to Egypt and others say it was the Midianites? Who is God referring to beside himself when he says, "Let *us* make human beings in our own image"? Who was Melchizedek, and what, if anything, does Abraham's tithing to this enigmatic figure have to say to us today about donations to the church? The list could go on and on. A reading of Genesis will raise many questions in our minds that are not quickly and easily resolved. Indeed, a number of questions remain unanswered even after intensive study. One important principle of interpretation is to recognize that not all of our questions can be answered.

Very few people could read Genesis at all without scholarly intervention. Not many people have studied Hebrew; neither have they read the translations sweated and sometimes fought over by scholars who have not only studied Hebrew but also other related languages like Aramaic, Akkadian, Ugaritic, and Arabic, not to speak of the language of the early translations like Greek and Latin.

While some of you may protest, my guess is that most are well aware that there are questions of interpretation and the nature of Genesis is not always on the surface. With this in mind, we turn to a consideration of the principles that offer the most promise of helping us understand the message of the book of Genesis.

WHERE IS MEANING FOUND?

What does it mean to interpret a biblical text like Genesis? What is our goal of interpretation?

Those who study hermeneutics, the technical name for interpretation, know that this question is hotly contested. In this postmodern age some people even deny the very existence of meaning. I will leave the details of this debate for discussion elsewhere.[1] Here I will operate with the confidence that what we are pursuing is the intention of the author who is writing a text to us. The author has a purpose, a message, which he or she is trying to communicate to an audience. We are part of that audience, and through the writing we come into contact with the thought of another.[2]

However, reading the writings of other people is different from carrying on a conversation with them. In both cases an act of communication is taking place, but in a conversation we can ask for clarification or expansion. Quite simply, we can ask, What do you mean? when something is unclear. We don't have that luxury when it comes to another's writings, and the matter only becomes more complicated when the writing under discussion was written centuries, even millennia, ago in a language that is now not spoken by anyone, as is the case with the Hebrew language of the book of Genesis.[3]

We are "distanced" from the author of Genesis. The book was written ages ago in a language that no one speaks today in a culture that is foreign to us.[4] The latter point means that there are customs that are strange to us, that are not a part of our experience. It also has repercussions for our coming to grips with the form of the literature itself. Robert Alter, an important figure in the modern exploration of ancient Hebrew literary forms, reminds us: "Every culture, even every era in a particular culture, develops distinctive and sometimes intricate codes for telling its stories."[5]

The historical, cultural and literary distance we are at from the time of the author makes Genesis difficult to grasp without study. Indeed, one of the biggest mistakes we can make in interpretation is to read it as if it were written for us today. For instance, later we will criticize those who read Genesis 1—2 as if it was an apologetic against modern scientific understanding of the origins of the world (Darwin), when in actuality it was an apologetic against rival ancient understandings of creation (*Enuma Elish*).

But even though these are issues that we need to recognize, we still haven't named the most important cause of our sense that Genesis describes a foreign world to us—its theology. The world of Genesis fully embraces supernatural realities. The characters may struggle with God, but they certainly never question his existence. God acts in space and time; indeed he creates space and time. God speaks to people and directs them to act in very specific ways.

For modern Christian readers of Genesis, there is a sense that we are entering a strange world that is difficult to understand. We have a "testament gap." In Genesis we go back to the beginning of the human relationship with God. We read of animal sacrifices, divine commands to slaughter a human being, God warring on behalf of his people, his wiping out almost all of humanity, and we scratch our heads and ask how does this relate to the gospel of Jesus Christ?

For these reasons it is important for us, if we really want to uncover the meaning of the text, to become conscious of what we are doing as interpreters. In that spirit, I offer the following principles of interpretation that are relevant to the study of Genesis. Here I will do little more than list them, while the following chapters will utilize them in our study of the text itself.

PRINCIPLE 1. RECOGNIZE THE LITERARY NATURE OF THE BOOK OF GENESIS

The Bible is a sacred book, but it is a book. God didn't create a new means of communication in order to speak to his people. The Hebrew language was not invented especially for divine use; God spoke in a language the people already knew. The Bible is similar to other books, and so we should study it with many of the same issues in mind that we have for literature in general.

Question 1: What kind of book is Genesis? This is one of the most fundamental and important questions to ask about any book, including biblical books. It is the question of genre, and genre triggers our reading strategy. It makes a world of difference whether we identify Genesis as myth, parable, history, legend or a combination of these and other genres. We expect different things from a parable than we do from a history book. Furthermore, if we conclude that Genesis is in some sense a history, that doesn't end the genre question, because there are different types of history writing. The question of the genre of Genesis is not an easy one, and it is highly controversial. However, no reading of the book can proceed without making a genre identification. Most people do it without reflection, a dangerous procedure since an error in this area results in fundamental misunderstanding of the book's message. We will give consideration to the genre of Genesis in chapter three.

Question 2. How did ancient Hebrews tell stories? We cannot read Genesis without recognizing that we are sitting at the feet of a master storyteller. For now, we leave open whether these stories are history or fiction, but in either case they are gripping and compelling narratives. As Robert Alter has suggested, though, different cultures tell their stories in different ways. In order to enrich our understanding of the message of Genesis, we need to be conscious of the art of the ancient Hebrew storyteller. Included in this study will be an examination of the structure and style of the book. (We also will turn our attention to this subject in chapter three.)

Question 3. Was Genesis written at one time by a single person? This question is always important in the study of a literary composition, but it has been made much more crucial in the light of the history of scholarship of Genesis during the modern era. Even though the question of the literary unity of Genesis is bound up with the nature of the entire Pentateuch, we will keep our focus on Genesis.

The history of interpretation indicates that for centuries the book of Genesis was happily read as a literary and authorial unity. Indeed, it is likely that the vast majority of readers across the world today still read the book in this way.

However, if we are honest, a close reading of the book raises questions. We might ask why there are two accounts of the creation (Gen 1:1-2:4a; 2:4b-25), which, when compared, seem to assert a slightly different sequence of events. We might notice that there are stories that are vaguely similar to one another, for instance the three stories where a patriarch lies about the marital status of his wife (see Gen 12:10-20; 20:1-18; 26:1-11), and question whether such a thing actually happened on three separate occasions. Perhaps, some say, they are variants of the same basic story. In addition, the attentive reader might wonder why the group that takes Joseph to Egypt is called the Midianites (Gen 37:28) on occasion rather than Ishmaelites, as they usually are. These are just a token of the kind of questions that make us wonder whether one or more literary forces are at work in the production of the book of Genesis.

Even if our own close reading of the book doesn't demand such inquiry, the present majority view of biblical scholars might. In most college and seminary courses on Genesis today in the Western world, one of the first matters of business will be delineating the sources of the book. Indeed, many readers who have taken such a class will have a notion of what I am referring to when I list the following letters: J, E, D and P (see pp. 49-57).

Question 4. What can we learn about Genesis from comparable ancient Near Eastern literature? The stories of Genesis have analogues from the other Near Eastern cultures. Israel was not the only people from this general area and time period to present an account of creation or even a devastating flood.

There are many dimensions to comparing ancient literature, but the main point that becomes obvious as soon as we become aware of literature written in other Semitic (e.g., Akkadian and Ugaritic) and non-Semitic languages (e.g., Egyptian, Sumerian and Hittite) of the Near East is that God did not create a unique form of literature any more than he created a unique language to communicate his truths.

However, we must tread carefully here. Too often the similarities have lured scholars and others into thinking that the Bible is just a superficial reworking of, say, Mesopotamian literature. They fail to see the significant differences between rival creation accounts—that is, between the biblical account and those from the ancient Near East. As we study ancient Near Eastern literature, we will remain attentive to both the similarities and the differences. We will also inquire into the reasons for both. The important point that comes to the fore through this kind of study is that the Bible is a literature of antiquity and not modernity. This truth will have a great impact on our study. For instance, we will come to realize that the biblical creation accounts were not written in order to counter Darwinism but rather the *Enuma Elish* and other ancient ideas concerning who created creation.

PRINCIPLE 2. EXPLORE THE HISTORICAL BACKGROUND OF THE BOOK

As we will continue to see, the issues that we explore under the first principle concerning the literary nature of the book are intertwined with those connected to the second principle. However, here we will focus on issues related to the space and time events outside of Genesis.

My interest here exposes my belief that literary texts do point to a world outside of itself. In other words, we deny that texts are purely self-referential. In the first place they are the products of the times that produce them. Thus it is important to explore those times as best as can be determined. Furthermore, I believe it is possible for a literary text to accurately, though certainly not exhaustively, inform us about past happenings.

There are three significant questions we can ask of Genesis (and other ancient texts) in regard to its historical background:

Question 5. When was Genesis written? The answer to this question may be discovered with ease or great difficulty. We might end up with certainty or doubt concerning our conclusions. We may be able to find an exact date or a general date. However, in all cases it is important to do our best with the evidence that is presented to us.

We can see how this question is related to our conclusions (principle 1, question 3) concerning the unity of the book. It is conceivable that Genesis was not written at one particular moment but rather over a long period of time. It will be important to investigate that question and then try to understand the historical processes behind the different stages of the production of the book. Even if our conclusion ends up being vague (e.g., Genesis is a product of the entire Old Testament time period), it still is valuable as an important reminder: we need to read the book against an ancient Near Eastern background and not unconsciously interpret it in the light of contemporary customs and events.

Question 6. What does Genesis tell us about the past? A book like Genesis is not just produced in the past, it may also tell us something about the past. The extent to which a book intends to pass down information about its time depends on its genre, again showing a connection between literary and historical concerns in interpretation. If Genesis turns out to be a parable or myth, we shouldn't expect it to inform us about what actually happened.

However, even if a book intends to be historical, this does not assure us that it does so accurately. Not all ancient historical writing has stood up to critical analysis. Indeed, there is a school of thought (minimalism) that suggests that all ancient writings, particularly the Bible, is ideologically biased and should not be trusted to give us a window on actual events.

However, even with those who are less skeptical about the connection between ancient texts and history, there are questions about the historical veracity of a book like Genesis. Why should this book be trusted to tell us what actually happened at the time of the patriarchs or Joseph in Egypt, and how in the world could a human author know anything about creation? These questions raise even further questions about how we learn about the past, the connection between the text and archeological research, and so forth.

Question 7. Does our knowledge of the ancient Near East help us understand Genesis? Earlier we raised the possibility that ancient Near Eastern materials might provide help in the area of literary analysis. We also gain information about the history of the region from select texts that have been discovered through archaeological exploration. Such information may concern both the time period in which the book was written as well as the time period that the book describes.

We are interested in not just extrabiblical confirmation but also setting the story of Genesis in the light of a broader historical context. To do so we will have to do our best to situate the biblical account in relationship to the history of the area, and we will hope to give a general sense of when these things happened in absolute terms.

A cursory reading of Genesis gives us some hope that such a study will be beneficial. After all, we read about Abraham leaving Ur, a city well known from ancient Near Eastern records. Later we hear that he fights against four kings from the east (Gen 14). Joseph rises to prominence in the Egyptian court. Perhaps connections can be drawn, at least to some extent.

There is yet a third way that ancient Near Eastern materials might help us to better understand the narratives of Genesis, and this is through the use of comparative customs. As we deal with the patriarchs, we will examine the oft-discussed relationship between their customs and those discovered from the ancient texts of Nuzi and Mari (see chap. 6).

Finally, a study of ancient Near Eastern literature brings us closer to the ancient worldview shared by Israel. It helps us recapture the strangeness of the Old Testament world, reminding us that it was not written yesterday but centuries ago.

PRINCIPLE 3. REFLECT ON THE THEOLOGICAL TEACHING OF THE BOOK

The Bible claims to be God's self-revelation to his people. Thus it would not be wrong to describe the theological message of the book as its most important feature. In essence, the Bible's primary purpose is to picture God and our relationship with him.

However, we must immediately qualify this statement so it is not abused. It is not uncommon today for scholars to make this assertion in order to minimize or even ignore the historical significance of the text. To say that theology is the most important aspect of the text is not to say that history is unimportant. Indeed, the Bible's consistent witness is that the God of the Bible acts in history. The book of Genesis is not a history-like story but rather a story-like history.

Though I am separating them here in order to facilitate our study, the literary (principle 1), historical (principle 2) and theological (principle 3) aspects of the text are all intertwined. The God of Genesis is one who reveals himself to his people (theology) in space and time (history) and who chooses to inspire writings that serve as a memorial of those events (literary).

However, since we are especially concerned in this section with theological issues, we will ask how God presents himself in relationship to his people.

Question 8. How does Genesis describe God? Theoretically, God could have chosen a number of different ways to reveal himself to us in a written text. He could have inspired the writing of a philosophical or theological essay. The text could have taken the form of a description of God's attributes. Like a traditional systematic theology, it might have reflected on God's omniscience, omnipresence and omnipotence. We might have received a learned and abstract analysis of the nature of God's being. But we did not. What we have in the Bible (and in Genesis) are stories and poems that tell us about God's involvement in the world. Granted that Genesis is for the most part prose and not poetry (though note Gen 49 and a number of smaller poetic pieces), like much of the rest of the Bible it does not describe God in abstract ways but tells us how God acts in the world.

Thus we learn about God not as a force but as a person. God is a person who creates, involves himself with his creation and rescues and judges his human creatures. To find out about God and his relationship with his people, we hear how he acts.

Even so, it appears that the book of Genesis strains at the task of revealing God to us. After all, how can the indescribable be described? The answer suggested in Genesis 1 is that human beings are created in the very image and likeness of God (Gen 1:26-27). An image is not the same as that which it images; thus it is wrong to think that the phrase "image of God" implies that human beings share in the divine nature. But it does suggest that, just as a statue of a king reflects his image, human beings reflect something of the nature of God. We are not surprised then that the descriptions of God in Genesis and elsewhere in the Bible are often humanlike.

Genesis 3, for instance, describes God as "walking" in the Garden. Does that mean that the author thought that God had legs? I don't think so. Rather, it was a way of conveying the thought that God had an intimate relationship with the first couple. In other words, it is an anthropomorphism, a description of God in human terms, terms that we know.

Anthropomorphisms belong to a broader category that is relevant to our study of how Genesis (and the Bible generally) depicts God: *metaphor* (a term under which I subsume simile). A metaphor is a comparison between two things that are essentially dissimilar, though the comparison is made to highlight an area that is similar. To call a person's teeth pearls is not to say they are round or of a certain size, it is to compliment their whiteness. To say that God is an intoxicated soldier (Ps 78:65) is not to say that he drinks wine or can get drunk; in the context it suggests that like an intoxicated soldier aroused from a alcohol-induced sleep, he will be irritated and dangerous.

Studying the theology of Genesis includes being on the lookout for metaphors of God. What are the implications of his being described as king, warrior, shepherd, guest or sojourner? To draw out those implications, we must unpack the metaphors. While this book is not the place to do so exhaustively, we will be attentive to many of the major ones, including that of a king who enters into a covenant with his people, which leads us to our next question.

Question 9. How does Genesis describe God's relationship to his people? So God is personal, and his nature and actions are often described by metaphors. Of the major metaphors used in the Bible to describe God, many of them are relational. A warrior implies an army, a shepherd implies a flock of sheep, a guest implies a host, and a king implies subjects. The task of theology is not just to ask questions about the nature and actions of God but also about the quality of God's relationship with his people. Thus we will explore the human side of the relationship as well.

In this regard, one particular metaphor deserves special mention: the covenant. *Covenant* is a particularly important and pervasive theme in Genesis. It first becomes explicit in Genesis 9 in reference to the relationship established between God and Noah, and then later is used in regard to the association between God and Abraham (Gen 15 and 17). The concept may also be implied elsewhere, but simply based on its use with Noah and Abraham it is clear that covenant is an important idea. When it is realized that covenant is also used extensively throughout the Old Testament, not to speak of the New Testament, we understand its importance even more profoundly.

When we properly understand the concept of covenant in the light of its ancient setting, we recognize that it has the form of a political treaty. The covenant in essence is like an ancient treaty between a king and his people. It not only makes clear the power structure of the relationship, but it also is the vehicle through which the king issues his will (law) to his people. We will pay attention to the development of this theological idea as well as others in the book of Genesis.

Question 10. How does Genesis fit into the whole of Scripture? As presently received by the Christian church, the book of Genesis is not an isolated entity. Indeed, it never was, considering that it is really the first chapter of a five part literary work known as the Torah or Pentateuch. However, my present point entails more than the fact that it is a part of the Torah.

Canon refers to the status of certain books that have been recognized as authoritative by the church through the ages. These books are considered to be the standard of faith and practice for the believing community. The belief is grounded in the fact that these books attest to their own ultimate divine authorship.[6] This assertion does not deny that that are a variety of human authors, styles and messages, but the final authority is grounded in an origin with God himself. Thus we legitimately have an expectation that the message of the whole coheres in an organic unity. An exciting aspect of biblical study is to recognize the rich diversity as well as the staggering coherence of its message.

The reality, nature and consequences of that coherence are much debated in contemporary scholarship these days.[7] However, this book is not the place to enter into that complex discussion. Accordingly, I will simply present the perspective that I think is most persuasive and fruitful, and allow you to judge its merits on its own.

The coherence of the Bible is grounded in the ultimate divine authorship of the whole. Thus in spite of a variety of styles, genres, themes and motifs, it's important to ask how the part (in this case the book of Genesis) fits into the whole (the Old and New Testaments). We begin with the recognition that Genesis provides the foundation. The rest of the Bible is built on that foundation. In other words, Genesis lays the foundation for the history of God's redemption of the world. It's not only the first chapter of the Pentateuch, but it is the first chapter of all the books that narrate God's ways in the world. We recognize this in the fact that Joshua picks up where the Pentateuch ends. Indeed, the Pentateuch ends with no strong sense of closure. The story must continue, and it continues in Joshua and is carried even further in Judges, Ruth, Samuel, Kings, Chronicles, Ezra, Nehemiah and Esther. In other words, Genesis initiates an Old Testament history of redemption that begins at creation and ends with the return from the exile and a description of the early diaspora.

But the Old Testament itself ends without a strong sense of closure and with an openness to the future. The testimony of Ezra, Nehemiah and Esther, as well as prophetic nonhistorical books like Daniel, Zechariah and Malachi, describe the people of God living in oppression. But it also describes those who are oppressed as living in the light of the sure hope of a future redemption. The New Testament describes the advent of that hoped for redemption.

With that background, we now turn to the words of Jesus Christ himself. He pointedly instructs his disciples in Old Testament interpretation. Perhaps we should not be surprised that Jesus instructs his disciples concerning this important aspect of hermeneutics. What is startling is that so few followers of Jesus today embrace their Lord's perspective on interpreting the Old Testament—and consequently Genesis. After his resurrection Jesus walks unrecognized with two disciples on the road to Emmaus. They are dumbfounded concerning the events that have just happened in

Jerusalem. They are in disbelief that Jesus has died on the cross. Then Jesus says to them:

> *"How foolish you are, and how slow of heart to believe all that the prophets have spoken! Did not the Christ have to suffer these things and then enter his glory?" And beginning with Moses and all the Prophets, he explained to them what was said in all the Scriptures concerning himself.* (Lk 24:25-27 NIV)

And then a little later, he spoke in a similar vein to a broader group of disciples:

> *"This is what I told you while I was still with you: Everything must be fulfilled that is written about me in the Law of Moses, the Prophets and the Psalms."*
>   *Then he opened their minds so they could understand the Scriptures. He told them, "This is what is written: The Christ will suffer and rise from the dead on the third day, and repentance and forgiveness of sins will be preached in his name to all nations, beginning at Jerusalem. You are witnesses of these things. I am going to send you what my Father has promised; but stay in the city until you have been clothed with power from on high."* (Lk 24:44-49 NIV)

Jesus' point is clear. The Old Testament anticipates his coming suffering and glorification. In both passages Jesus instructs his disciples that the entire Old Testament proclaims his coming. In the first passage he cites "Moses and all the Prophets" and in the second passage he refers to "the Law of Moses, the Prophets and the Psalms." Both these phrases were used to refer to what we call the Old Testament (which was not used as a title until the New Testament came into existence).

Our concern in this book is with Genesis, the first book of the law of Moses. Jesus thus invites us to consider the possibility that the message of Genesis somehow anticipates his future ministry.

This passage in Luke 24 raises the debated question of the role of the New Testament in the interpretation of the Old. Many scholars defend the idea that Christian interpretation of the Old Testament must never appeal to the New Testament. They honestly feel that such a move distorts the meaning of the more ancient text. On the contrary, and on the basis of Jesus' instruction in Luke 24, I submit that it is wrong for a Christian to ignore the good news of Christ in the act of interpreting the Old Testament and, for our purposes, the book of Genesis.

To be sure, when we begin our interpretation, it's important to ask how the original audience would have understood the Old Testament passage under study, and it's not my contention that the full significance of the text's relationship to Christ would have been recognized by an ancient reader (or the author for that matter).[8] Though it is true that there was a messianic expectation at the time of Christ, the actual shape of his advent was a surprise to most, even the most ardent reader of the Hebrew Bible. However, once Christ had fulfilled the Old Testament, a Christian cannot and should not resist seeing *how* he fulfilled it. The Christ event enriches our understanding of the message of the Old Testament.

An analogy may help. When we read a good mystery (or see one at the movie theater) for the first time, we may find that opening events and dialogue have a meaning that is not clear until we reach the conclusion. We cannot read a good mystery the same way a second time. There will always be a sense of "Oh yes, now I see the significance of that event." Or for the Old Testament, "Yes, indeed, this does point to the coming of Christ."

Right now, our discussion is all very general and vague. However, as we engage the text of Genesis I will demonstrate how Genesis, when read in the context of the finished canon, may be seen to point to Christ. It certainly lays the foundation of the redemptive history that is fulfilled with his coming (see, for instance, chap. 10).

Question 11. What in Genesis is theologically normative for today? Many Bible readers start with this question. This is understandable. After all, it's the proper goal of our efforts. We want to know how the Word of God affects our life. How does a passage address my beliefs, and how does it shape my actions today?

This admirable enthusiasm for knowing God and his will today, however, can lead to a serious misconstrual of God's message. Without the hard work entailed in the preceding questions and principles, we are much more likely to mishear the Word of God.

This is particularly the case with the Old Testament. The Old Testament is much more difficult for modern Christian readers to understand than the New. We are further distanced chronologically, culturally and in terms of redemptive history from the events of the Old Testament. Indeed, even with careful study and an awareness of the interpretive principles, our study of Genesis will not escape difficulty. We should be prepared to recognize when our interpretations are certain, merely probable or even tenuous. The more certain we are that Genesis teaches something that remains normative for our belief and behavior today, the more firmly we should embrace it. On the other hand, if our understanding is tenuous, we shouldn't consider the point essential. We will later see that some of the most vociferous debates about Genesis (for instance, the length of the creation days) are based on fairly tenuous interpretations. It's a good principle to operate with the belief that what God considers essential for our relationship with him is taught clearly and in many places; in other words we can't miss it if we tried. On the other hand, while it is still valuable to try to discover all that we can of what the Bible teaches, we must learn to "not sweat the small stuff" in biblical interpretation as well as in life.

PRINCIPLE 4. REFLECT ON YOUR SITUATION, YOUR SOCIETY'S SITUATION AND THE GLOBAL SITUATION

To know how to apply the Bible to our lives and our world, we must be aware of ourselves and our surroundings. It is certainly possible to overdo this, but most of us are not as reflective as we should be. Sure, we know where we experience joy and pain in our lives, but most of us need to go deeper in our self-awareness. What are my relationships like, and can I discern patterns in my relationships with others? What do I admire in other people, and what do I detest or feel indifferent toward? Why? What about the past? Have there been events that have shaped me for good or bad?

The list can go on, but the simple and often neglected truth is that the best interpreters of the Bible are those who not only can read the Bible but can read themselves, others and the world at large. Without this knowledge it is impossible to bridge the ancient world of the text to the modern world we live in. Without that bridging we have not completed the hermeneutical, or interpretive, task. What is vitally important is, What does Genesis mean to us today? However, we must first figure out what it meant to Moses before we can proceed to that final step.

Question 12. *What is my redemptive-historical relationship to the events of Genesis?* The book of Genesis records events that happened in the far distant past. Its purview stretches from creation down through the time of the patriarchs. While the Bible does not give us the information we need to date the creation, we may safely situate the patriarchs roughly in the first half of the second millennium B.C.

Genesis was written long ago, and a lot of water has passed under the bridge. God's strategy of redemption has flowed from these events through the exodus and conquest, the period of the judges and kings, and the exile and postexilic period. The New Testament gives testimony to the climactic event of Christ's death and resurrection and the founding and early history of the church. We live on the far side of all these events. As part of our task of appropriating the message of Genesis, we must ask how the book's stories relate to us today. How are we related to the Noahic and Abrahamic covenant? What do we do with the picture of God's warring activity in Genesis 14? The questions are endless.

The attentive reader can see that this question is intimately connected with my comments on theology where I asked how the book fits into the canon as a whole. I revisit it here to remind us that an important aspect of bringing the text to bear in the twenty-first century has to do with an awareness of our redemptive-historical relationship with the events recorded therein.

Question 13. *What can I learn from Genesis about how to think and act in a way pleasing to God?* The Bible not only helps us situate ourselves in redemptive history, but it also guides our moral and intellectual life. While it is true that the book of Genesis does not do so in as direct a way as, say, the law in Exodus 19—24 or Proverbs (though even here there are issues of continuity and discontinuity), its stories intend to form the believer's worldview and provide illustrations of proper behavior.

As the first book of the canon Genesis begins to lay down a worldview for its readers. That is, it provides foundational teaching that provides a lens through which we interpret our experience of the world. By way of illustration, I might point to the first chapter of the book. Here we are introduced to a God who is not a part of his creation (he is transcendent) but is involved with it (immanent). Everything is dependent on God, who created it, and he created it good. Human beings are not the most important thing in the cosmos (God is), but we have a special relationship with him, and that confers dignity on us (image of God). These truths are not something we would come to apart from the revelation of Genesis, and they are important for how we think about the world and act toward it.

But Genesis does more than form a worldview; it also teaches us how to behave. It is appropriate to read the stories of Adam and Eve, Cain, Noah, Abraham, Jacob, Joseph, and the other characters as illustrative of moral principles. Later we will develop the plot of the Abraham narrative as a journey of faith, and his journey throws light on the ups and downs in our own relationship with God. Joseph's response to the seductions of Potiphar's wife is a model of obedience that intends to guide other men (and women) when faced with the same temptation. In other words, there is a sense in which we can read the text and say to ourselves or to others "Go, and do likewise." On the other hand, there are also counterillustrations—the rebellion of Adam and Eve, the fratricide of Cain, the deceptions of Jacob, the murderous intent of Joseph's brothers—that should elicit a "Go, and don't do likewise."

Although most sermons on the Old Testament today take this approach, many people resist it, saying that the purpose of these narratives are theological and not moral. Of course, such a reaction insists on a false dichotomy. God intends us to read Genesis both theologically and morally.

However, it is not as simple as reading the text and simply applying it to our lives. In Genesis Abraham is told that he and his descendants, the godly, must circumcise their sons on the eighth day. "Go, and do likewise?" Not in this case. Why? Because the New Testament tells us that circumcision is a ritual connected to the old covenant. Of course we may choose to circumcise our sons, but for other than religious reasons. Abraham went to war against the kings of the east who kidnapped Lot, and Abraham was victorious because God fought with him. Does this mean that God fights along with his people today? Not necessarily. It's important to ask questions about issues of continuity and discontinuity. It's also important, and sometimes difficult to take into account ancient customs that are not meant to be normative but were part of the culture of the day. Courting rituals (Gen 24) may be a case in point. It is not at all clear that God intends his people today to follow tribal courting practices of the early second millennium B.C. These issues involve reflection rather than immediate application.

Though I can't be exhaustive here, in the chapters that follow I will model the proper way to appropriate the text of Genesis to our lives today.

Question 14: How can I keep from imposing my own views on Genesis? Once we realize that we have to work at the interpretive process, we might fear that the text is open to a number of different interpretations. If this is true, why should we trust the one we have come to? We might be fooling ourselves.

In the first place, it is important to adopt humility in our interpretation. We must acknowledge that it is possible that we are wrong, so we must be open to other interpretations. We should test our understanding of Genesis by "reading in community." Protestants sometimes lose sight of the importance of this because our movement was founded by breaking away from the tyranny of official church interpretation and insisting on the priesthood of all believers. But there is a middle ground between "It's between God and me" and simply submitting to the authoritative interpretation of others. We need to wrestle with the text on our own and then expose ourselves to the thinking of others. Indeed, we should seek out opinions of people who may have opinions different from our own. As a middle-aged, white, relatively well-off male, I want to hear women speak about the text. I want to read commentaries by Asian, African (American), Latino scholars and pastors. I want to be exposed to the thoughts of other Ph.D.s as well as people with no education. Why? Not because the text is flexible but because different people will attend to different things in the text. "Reading in community" is done by joining Bible study groups and Sunday School classes, listening to sermons, reading commentaries, and so forth. The comments that I make on Genesis have been enriched by many years of listening to others talk about their understanding of the book.

CONCLUSION: HOW IN THE WORLD
CAN I DO ALL OF THIS?

I hope that after you have read this chapter, I have convinced you that deep reflection on the literary, theological and historical nature of Genesis is important to understanding the ancient message and applying it to today. However, for many the task will appear daunting. So I would like to make a few final comments of encouragement.

First, no one fathoms the entire depth or breadth of meaning of the biblical text. The message is too rich. Rather than being discouraging, I think this ought to encourage all of us. It means that even our first understandings of the text are worthwhile. The most important aspects of the book are taught so clearly and repeatedly that they are hard to miss. And there are always new dimensions of the book to discover. Realizing this energizes continued reading.

Second, none of us can or have to do all the work. We can gain help from others who have devoted their lives to the study of the Bible and its background. Very few people can become experts in ancient Near Eastern backgrounds, for instance, but those who do have written books alerting us to the material that is available. Commentaries should never be used as a means of avoiding our own personal reflection, but they should not be ignored either.[9]

It is my hope that this book will not only articulate principles helpful for interpreting Genesis but also model their application. To that task we now turn.

SUMMARY OF THE INTERPRETIVE QUESTIONS

1. What kind of book is Genesis?

2. How did ancient Hebrews tell stories?

3. Was Genesis written at one time by a single person?

4. What can we learn about Genesis from comparable ancient Near Eastern literature?

5. When was Genesis written?

6. What does Genesis tell us about the past?

7. Does our knowledge of the ancient Near East help us understand Genesis?

8. How does Genesis describe God?

9. How does Genesis describe God's relationship to his people?

10. How does Genesis fit into the whole of Scripture?

11. What in Genesis is theologically normative for today?

12. What is my redemptive-historical relationship to the events of Genesis?

13. What can I learn from Genesis about how to think and act in a way pleasing to God?

14. How can I keep from imposing my own views on Genesis?

FOR FURTHER READING

Fee, Gordon D., and Douglas Stuart. *How to Read the Bible for All Its Worth*. 3rd ed. Grand Rapids: Zondervan, 2003.

Klein, William W., Craig L. Blomberg and Robert L. Hubbard. *Introduction to Biblical Interpretation*. Nashville: Thomas Nelson, 1993.

Longman, Tremper, III. *Reading the Bible with Heart and Mind*. Colorado Springs: NavPress, 1997.

Silva, Moisés, ed. *Foundations of Contemporary Interpretation*. Grand Rapids: Zondervan, 1996.

Vanhoozer, Kevin J. *Is There a Meaning in This Text?* Grand Rapids: Zondervan, 1998.

Wenham, Gordon J. *Story as Torah: Reading the Old Testament Narrative Ethically*. Grand Rapids: Baker, 2004.

P A R T

READING GENESIS
AS LITERATURE

■   ■   ■

Most Christians read Genesis for theological, historical, devotional and practical reasons. It's easy to forget that it is a literary work. Indeed, most scholars today would judge it, along with the books of Samuel, as the high point of ancient Israelite narrative literature.

However, this judgment has not always ruled the day. Indeed, most scholarly attention has been directed toward dissecting the book into hypothetical source material rather than coming to understand the book as a coherent whole. Attitudes regarding this have changed over the past twenty years, but there are still many questions about whether or not Genesis is a literary masterpiece, a jumbled patchwork of sources or both. We will address this issue in chapter two.

In chapter three, we move from issues of compositional history to an analysis of the final form of the book. What kind of book is Genesis? History, myth, folktale? And then what are the stylistic features that make Genesis such a powerful story?

TWO

WHO WROTE GENESIS?

What is the origin of the book of origins (Genesis)? It may surprise most readers that this seemingly simple question has generated intense passion for over one hundred years. How we answer this question often leads to a quick assessment of our orthodoxy. Deny that Moses wrote the Pentateuch and some will suspect your allegiance to the faith. Affirm that Moses wrote the Pentateuch and others will question your intelligence.

Such strongly held views are perplexing in the light of the fact that Genesis nowhere names an author or describes the process of its composition. What are we to make of it all?

DID MOSES WRITE GENESIS?

The issue is presently more complicated than it has ever been in the past. Rival theories have proliferated, but we can boil the controversy down to the question, Did Moses compose the book of Genesis?

Genesis is technically an anonymous book; that is, it nowhere names its author. However, we need to expand the search for an author to include the entire Pentateuch, since the first five books of the Old Testament present themselves as a coherent unit. Even so, nowhere within the Pentateuch does Moses or anyone else claim to have written it. If this is the case, what is the evidence that supports the idea that Moses wrote Genesis?

First, elsewhere in the Pentateuch we hear that Moses was a recipient of revelation and a witness to redemptive acts. Furthermore, on occasion we read that he wrote down certain historical events (Ex 17:14; Num 33:2), laws (Ex 24:4; 34:27) as well as a song (Deut 31:22; see Deut 32). While this evidence is far from convincing concerning the authorship of the Pentateuch as a whole (and even more for Genesis), it does raise difficult questions for those people who say that Moses had nothing to do with its composition, particularly in the case of the law, which the text tells us he received and transmitted to future generations. If this depiction proved to be fictional, serious theological questions would arise. In such a case, if the text is trying to establish the authority of the law in part on its promulgation by the revered Moses, then why should we accept a law presented in a fraudulent manner?

Besides the inner-Pentateuchal references to Moses' writing activity, very early in biblical history a tradition arose that connected the Pentateuch with Moses. Scholars will disagree over the dates of the following biblical texts, but just mentioning them is informative.

The first example comes from Joshua 1. Moses is dead and Joshua is in charge of the Israelites as they prepare to enter the Promised Land. God encourages Joshua at this critical and potentially dangerous moment with the following charge:

> You are the one who will lead these people to possess all the land I swore to their ancestors I would give them. Be strong and very courageous. Be careful to obey all the instructions Moses gave you. Do not deviate from them, turning either to the right or to the left. Then you will be successful in everything you do. (Josh 1:6-7)

While the reference to the "instructions Moses gave you" probably points more specifically to the laws in Exodus to Deuteronomy, it does indicate that Moses bequeathed some textual tradition to the following generations.

Later in the history of Israel, the Israelites could refer to a "book of

Moses" (2 Chron 25:4; Ezra 6:18; Neh 13:1). These passages provide strong intrabiblical data for a Mosaic writing, while not being specific about its shape or scope. It's also clear that Jesus and the early church connected much, if not all, of the Torah with Moses (Mt 19:7; 22:24; Mk 7:10; 12:26; Jn 1:17; 5:46; 7:23).

While it is true that none of these references refer specifically to material found in Genesis, it does connect Moses with the composition of the later books of the Pentateuch, to which Genesis serves as a preamble. We should not be surprised to learn that until the past couple hundred years there was little doubt in the church or synagogue that Moses was the author of Genesis.

PROBLEMS WITH MOSAIC AUTHORSHIP

Even so, attentive readers of the Pentateuch know that there are items included about which Moses could not have known. The flagship example of these so-called post-Mosaica is the account of the death of Moses in Deuteronomy 34. Moses could not have written the record of his death, and attempts to ground the chapter in a prophetic revelation are strained.

But there are more such items that are easily detected when we know something of the history of Israel. For example, the town in Mesopotamia from which Abraham came to the Promised Land is called "Ur of the Chaldeans" (Gen 11:28, 31; 15:7). No one doubts the antiquity of Ur. It was an ancient city, founded long before Moses and Abraham before him. It is the qualifier, "of the Chaldeans," that is universally recognized as coming after Moses. The Chaldeans were a first-millennium-B.C. Aramaic-speaking tribe that came to dominate southern Mesopotamia (now southern Iraq) including the area of Ur. The reason why the additional identification is given is because there were other cities and villages named Ur (including one that was in the area today controlled by the nation of Syria). The reference to the Chaldeans helped a first-millennium readership understand which particular city their ancestor came from.

Yet another example comes from Genesis 14. The chapter concerns a raid by a group of four eastern kings who, among other things, capture Abraham's nephew Lot and intend to take him back with them. Abraham sets out in hot pursuit to save his kinsman. Genesis 14:14 begins this part of the story: "When Abram heard that his nephew Lot had been captured, he mobilized the 318 trained men who had been born into his household. Then he pursued Kedorlaomer's army until he caught up with them in Dan." Most readers would pass over the reference to Dan without pause; however, if we think about it, we might remember that the city of Dan is named after Abraham's great-grandson. We even have the story where this city is named Dan (Judg 17—18). The city existed during Abraham's time period, but at that time its name was Laish. Someone changed the name so later generations could understand exactly where this place was.

Other concrete examples could be given, but the principle is clear. There are indications of post-Mosaic activity in the book of Genesis (and beyond). What is not clear is exactly how extensive the later editing is. We notice the obvious changes, but are these the only ones, or are they the tip of a very big iceberg?

OBVIOUS SOURCES

There is strong evidence that parts of Genesis (and the Pentateuch) were written after the death of Moses. Now we turn our attention briefly to the evidence that parts of Genesis were written before Moses. Or, more accurately, parts of the book are treated as sources that are woven into the main fabric of the book.

First we need to remember what the contents of Genesis are. Genesis is a narration of events from the moment of creation down to the death of Joseph. It's clear that these are accounts of things that happened long before Moses. How did Moses know about them to write about them?

For those who affirm the reality of divine revelation, we must consider the possibility that God told Moses what happened and that Moses wrote down what he heard or saw. However, an appeal to direct auditory or visionary revelation is not a necessary or elegant hypothesis, and in any case there is explicit evidence for another approach, namely, that Moses used sources that were passed down through the generations.

The most blatant evidence for sources is the so-called *toledot* formulas. These are sentences that begin with the Hebrew phrase *'elleh toledot*, which has been translated in a number of ways, including "these are the generations," "this is the family history" and "this is the account." The phrase is always followed by a personal name (with the exception of the first occurrence, which names instead the "heavens and the earth," Gen 2:4). The person named is not necessarily the main character but only the beginning point of the section of the book that also closes with the person's death. There are eleven such formulas, and these provide introductions to sections of Genesis that were likely original sources passed down the generations and included in the final book. These eleven *toledot* also structure the book and serve to define it as a prologue (1:1—2:3) followed by various episodes: the "generations of" Adam (5:1), Noah (6:9), Noah's sons (10:1), Shem (11:10), Terah (11:27), Isaac (25:19), Esau (36:1, 9) and Jacob (37:2). That these sources were likely written by the time they came down to Moses may be seen in the reference to the "book *[sefer]* of the *toledot* of Adam." However, we really do not know the details of transmission of these ancient sources of knowledge, and therefore we aren't sure whether they were all written or some were oral and the others written.

In any case the conclusion is clear; if Moses was the author, he utilized sources in Genesis in order to learn about events that happened long before he was born.

INDICATIONS OF MULTIPLE AUTHORSHIP

Following the evidence provided by the biblical text itself, we are now on firm ground to make the following three assertions:

1. The tradition of Moses writing the Pentateuch points to his role as an important, foundational figure in its composition.

2. There most likely was editorial activity after Moses.

3. Sources most likely were available to Moses concerning the events that happened in Genesis.

Many who study and write about Genesis, however, go further and assert that that there are indications that rather than thinking of an author who uses sources and whose writing is later edited, the evidence points to multiple authors who are in tension and even contradict each other.

I will begin with what can be classified as a minor example of the type of evidence that leads many to draw this conclusion. Though minor, it is telling. The text in question occurs in the context of Genesis 37, the story of Joseph's sale to a merchant caravan on its way to Egypt.

> *As they [the brothers of Joseph] sat down to eat their meal, they looked up and saw a caravan of* Ishmaelites *coming from Gilead. Their camels were loaded with spices, balm and myrrh, and they were on their way to take them down to Egypt.*
>
> *Judah said to his brothers, "What will we gain if we kill our brother and cover up his blood? Come, let's sell him to the* Ishmaelites *and not lay our hands on him; after all, he is our brother, our own flesh and blood." His brothers agreed.*
>
> *So when the* Midianite *merchants came by, his brothers pulled Joseph up out of the cistern and sold him for twenty shekels of silver to the* Ishmaelites, *who took him to Egypt. (Gen 37:25-28 NIV, emphasis added)*

To whom did the brothers sell Joseph, the Ishmaelites or the Midianites? At first the passage, if read closely, is quite jarring. Those who believe that the book of Genesis is the construction of originally separate sources take this alternating between names as evidence that there were at least two stories of Joseph's sale, one with Ishmaelites and another with Midianites.

A more dramatic and significant example of what some students of Genesis believe is compelling evidence for more than one source are the two apparently separate and different accounts of creation. The first account is found in Genesis 1:1—2:4a, which is structurally rigid and formal in presentation as it recounts the events of the six days of creation and the seventh of rest. The second creation story (Gen 2:4b-25) has the shape of an interesting and compelling story with a focus on the first human pair in the Garden of Eden. What leads some to conclude that these are two separate creation accounts is the evidence of tension, even contradiction, between the two accounts. For instance, according to Genesis 1, vegetation came into being on the third day, while humans were formed on the sixth. In Genesis 2, humans were created when "neither wild plants nor grains were growing on the earth" (Gen 2:5).

These are just two examples of what many would say are hundreds or even thousands of indications of tension and contradiction in the content of the Pentateuch. Such evidence has typically led to alternative understandings of the composition of Genesis and the Pentateuch.

AN ALTERNATIVE THEORY OF THE COMPOSITION OF GENESIS

One problem with describing alternative theories of the composition of Genesis (and the Pentateuch) is that there are so many variants of the idea. There is no unanimity among those who are convinced that Genesis was composed by bringing together different traditions. However, I will describe what most people recognize as the historically most powerful theory, acknowledge variations on this theory, and point to some of the most cogent recent permutations of the theory. After this I will criticize the whole enterprise and then reiterate what I think is the best understanding of the compositional history of Genesis.

THE DOCUMENTARY HYPOTHESIS

One of the most dramatic dates in the history of modern biblical interpretation is 1883 with the publication of the German edition of *The Prolegomena to the History of Israel* by Julius Wellhausen (English translation in 1885). Wellhausen did not come up with a totally new idea; his work was the capstone on ideas that had been percolating for over a century. However, his book put a twist on a theory of the composition of the Pentateuch, and he convinced the vast majority of his fellow scholars in Germany, England and the United States. I am presenting his perspective on the issue not because everyone (or even anyone) today exactly agrees with his position, but because his views were dominant until the 1980s, and the vast majority of theories that depart from the affirmation of essential Mosaic authorship are really variants of this viewpoint.

Identifying factors. Four observations trigger the hypothesis that the Pentateuch is the weaving together of four separate sources:

1. The use of different divine names, particularly Yahweh and Elohim. This first observation led to the initial separation of two sources, one that used Yahweh, and thus received the name J, for Jahwist (as the Germans spelled it), and the second that used Elohim, the generic term for God, and thus received the name E, for Elohist.

2. *The use of two or more different names to designate the same person, tribe or place.* We have already seen an example of this in the alternation of Ishmaelites and Midianites in Genesis 37. Elsewhere we find that Moses' father-in-law is called by three different names: Reuel, Jethro and Hobab. The mountain where God gives the law to Moses is usually called Sinai but occasionally it is called Horeb.

3. *The appearance of doublets.* This is similar to the previous point, but it's different enough to be listed separately. A doublet is the repetition of the same basic story, though different characters may be involved. Doublets could be repeated accounts (e.g., the wife-sister stories, Gen 12:10-20; 20; 26) or separate incidents serving the same purpose in the narrative context (e.g., Joseph's dreams of stars and sheaves, Gen 37:5-11).

4. *Different theologies.* In order to discern different theological emphases, a scholar would have to have already separated the sources from one another. Once that is done in a preliminary fashion, distinctive perspectives on the nature of God or the religious institutions can be used to further delineate the sources. One of the more interesting examples is the progression among the sources in terms of form of worship, for example, the issue of centralization of worship. According to traditional criticism, J is unaware of centralization (Ex 20:24-26), D calls for it (Deut 12:1-26), and P assumes it (Ex 25-40; Numbers; and Lev 1—9).[1]

The sources. After close readings—some would argue too close— scholars discovered four separate sources in the Pentateuch, three of which are found specifically in the book of Genesis. These sources are best known by the letters J, E, D and P, and the documentary hypothesis is sometimes called the "JEDP hypothesis." In general, these four letters stand for the four particular traditions that developed in different times and places by Israelite theologians, and were woven together by redactors (another word for editor) to form the Pentateuch as we know it. Redactors honored each of these traditions by including them, perhaps not in their entirety, even though the resulting composition was filled with tensions and contradictions. Some of the original proponents of this theory felt that the "Semitic mind" was not as attentive to logical contradictions as the "German mind," but since World War II such statements repel us. However, such criticism of some motives behind the development of the hypothesis does not disqualify it, since today it is not just German Protestant scholars who hold this view, but many Catholic and Jewish scholars as well.

Once the four sources are identified, it's possible to provide a description of their main concerns and to suggest dates and places of origin. While there is much debate among advocates of the hypothesis, the following is a fair representation of its general outline.

J (Jahwist). J derives its name from the source that uses the name Yahweh most consistently. J is a storyteller, which is observed by comparing the tone of the second creation story in Genesis 2:4-25 with the first in 1:1—2:3 (which is assigned to P). J describes God using the human analogies: God walks in the Garden and has casual conversations with Adam and Eve, for instance. In J's theology God is not the only a god, but he is by far the most powerful god and the only one worthy of worship (this is called henotheism and is not monotheism). As opposed to P and D, God may be worshiped at many altars rather than at one central altar. J is thus the earliest source, perhaps coming from around the time of David and Solomon in the tenth-century B.C., and thus it emanates from theologians in Israel's south. Not so long ago the literary critic Harold Bloom caught the imagination of many educated laypeople by publishing a book suggesting that J should be identified with a woman, perhaps even David's granddaughter, which is as speculative as it is provocative.[2]

E (Elohist). The E source derives its name from its supposedly consistent use of the generic name for God, Elohim. Some scholars argue that E presumes the division of the kingdom after Solomon, and E texts should be associated with northern theologians, which would place it about one hundred years after J, though others doubt it.[3] Those who place its original composition in the north point to the important role that northern figures like Joseph (who of course never lived in the land, but his two sons give their names to prominent tribes in the north). E opens with Genesis 15 and continues here and there through Numbers 32, though a few passages in Deuteronomy are also assigned to E. Those who identify an E source recognize that it is much harder to detect and is at best fragmentary in the final form of the Pentateuch. An increasing number of scholars doubt that there is a separate E source, and they merge it in with J, which seems to belie the original reason for recognizing J, namely, its use of Yahweh as opposed to Elohim for God.

D (Deuteronomist). The D source is pretty much identical with the book of Deuteronomy; it is not woven in with the rest of the sources in the first four books. However, D as a source of the Pentateuch is often considered to be a linchpin to the dating of the other sources.[4] According to advocates of the theory, this source is able to be dated with pinpoint accuracy, thanks to the story found in 2 Kings 22—23.

In 2 Kings 22—23 we have the account of the reform of the corrupted religion of Israel performed by King Josiah of Judah. In the process of cleaning out the temple, the priests find a book, which, according to the narrative, had been suppressed.

Once the book is read, it becomes immediately clear that the people of God were not obeying its provisions. The fact that Josiah sets out to centralize the worship of Yahweh in Judah after this reading demonstrates that the document he was reading included Deuteronomy 12. Now whether Josiah's discovery was of the entire book or a portion of it is not clear from the narrative.

The text of Kings states that Josiah's people found a lost document. However, this text has been used by many source critics to suggest a date of composition for D. In other words, they believe that D was not found but was written at this point and was presented as a Mosaic document to garner the high authority they wanted it to receive, and thus they could control the shape of worship in Israel. That is, Josiah perpetrated a "pious fraud." For this reason, many advocates of the traditional documentary hypothesis feel that they can date D to the time of Josiah, the late-seventh-century B.C., specifically 621 B.C.

P (Priestly). In many ways P is the source that is easiest to pick out of the final product of the Pentateuch. Its concerns include chronology, genealogy, ritual, worship and law—areas easily associated with the priesthood, thus its name. However, as we will question later, even though it is easy to spot those sections that tend to be identified as priestly, there is still a question whether that is because this material is from a separate source (P) or that the content of the passage calls for a distinctive style.

Though much of the material is believed to have come from an earlier time, the collection known as P has traditionally been given a late date, in the fifth or the fourth century, and is related to the exile and after. P reflects the postexilic order of the priesthood and also that time period's concern with obedience to the law. One argument used to support the late date of the source is the fact that P shows influence only on Chronicles, a book dated to the fifth century at the earliest.[5]

P is detected extensively from Genesis to Numbers. Great portions of these books are assigned to P, as are a few verses of Deuteronomy. They can stand side-by-side with other material from other sources. The classic example of this is Genesis 1, the so-called first creation account, which is assigned to P, while the second, Genesis 2, is assigned to J. Sometimes, however, P interweaves with other sources (as in the traditional analysis of the flood narrative into J and P).

Summary of the documentary hypothesis. The documentary hypothesis has been the most potent rival to the traditional view that Moses was the fountainhead of the Pentateuch. In contrast with the latter view, the documentary hypothesis takes the Pentateuch completely out of the hands of Moses, which raises questions for many about the veracity and authority of Genesis and the Pentateuch. After all, though the Pentateuch does not claim Mosaic authorship, it at least depicts Moses as the recipient of large parts of the revelatory content, particularly the law. Even though the authority of the text is grounded in Yahweh himself rather than in Moses, we can't help but have doubts if uncertainty is cast on the Torah's picture of Moses as recipient of the law at Mount Sinai.

In any case, for over a century the documentary hypothesis has held sway among academics who study the Pentateuch. But the past twenty years have witnessed a significant erosion in its popularity. Even those who basically hold to a hypothetical source theory like the documentary hypothesis have great differences among themselves.

PROBLEMS WITH THE DOCUMENTARY HYPOTHESIS

After Wellhausen the great majority of scholars advocated the documentary hypothesis as the best explanation for the origin of Genesis (and the Pentateuch as a whole). However, there has never ceased to be prominent scholarly voices that have raised concerns about it.[6] These are mostly conservative Jewish and Christian scholars. More recently, however, nonconservatives like R. Norman Whybray, Isaac M. Kikawada and Arthur Quinn as well as other conservative scholars (Gordon J. Wenham and Kenneth A. Kitchen) have joined the chorus of uncertainty over this hypothesis.[7] The trend away from documentary analysis is attributable to two causes: (1) problems with the method, and (2) newer and more holistic approaches to the text. These two are closely related. The problems have encouraged interpreters toward a holistic reading of the text, and a holistic reading of the text accentuates the problems. Nonetheless, the two points will be described separately.

Recent years have seen a surge of doubt about the documentary hypothesis. In the first place, there is skepticism concerning the criteria used to separate the sources. Kitchen and others, for instance, have shown that multiple names for gods are commonplace in ancient Near Eastern texts about which we have no doubt concerning their literary coherence. The variation may result from stylistic practice rather than the presence of sources.

No one can deny the presence of doublets, similar or nearly similar stories, in Genesis. A quick reading of Genesis 12:10-20, 20:1-17 and 26:1-25 is convincing enough. In each text a patriarch protects himself in a foreign court by passing off his wife as his sister. Traditional criticism takes a source-critical approach and assigns the first and the last to J, and the middle story to E.[8] Recent study on Semitic literary style suggests that such repetitions were consciously employed in the literature to achieve a certain effect. Robert Alter's studies show that these doublets are actually "a purposefully deployed literary convention" that he names "type scenes." Alter defines a type scene as a commonly repeated narrative pattern in which the author highlights similarities in order to draw the reader's attention to the connection between the two stories.[9] Alter contrasts this literary solution to the presence of "couplets" over against the source hypothesis. He is content to highlight the literary connections between the stories. Those who believe that God acts purposefully in history can see his hand behind the text as he shapes the events himself.

We can easily discern the difference in style between the story-like J and the more list-oriented, formal P. However, is this a difference in authorship or a difference in subject matter? And if we grant a difference of authorship (or more precisely, the use of existing sources for, say, genealogies), on what grounds should P be dated later than J?

Concerning the presence of two names for some places, people or things, the solution is much the same as for doublets. The phenomenon has been noted in extrabiblical texts whose single authorship is beyond doubt. Also sometimes there is an explanation for the variation that undermines the hypothesis that there are two different sources being brought together. In regard to the variation of Ishmaelite and Midianite (Gen 37), closer examination shows that these are not two groups but rather one. Ishmaelite is a broader category of people among whom are the Midianites.[10]

The last criterion is that of theological differences. Virtually no one today accepts Julius Wellhausen's idea that in the pages of the Old Testament we can trace a religious evolution from animism to henotheism to monotheism (though there are statements that are both henotheistic and monotheistic in the text). His Hegelian presuppositions are well recognized and rejected by contemporary critics. Furthermore, Wellhausen was motivated by the Romantic desire to recover the ideal primitive past, and he applied this concept to his study of the Bible. Today's mindset is different. Even in the critical circles that are directly descended from Wellhausen, the focus of attention has shifted away from source analysis and toward the final form of the text. In addition, many of the theological differences that have been used to delineate sources may be interpreted in a different fashion and point in a different direction. For instance, going back to the issue of the centralization of worship there is no question but that the Pentateuch records different attitudes toward the central altar. It is true that Exodus 20 assumes more than one place of worship while

Deuteronomy 12 calls for centralization, and the texts in Leviticus and Numbers assume it. A close examination of Deuteronomy 12, however, indicates that the call was not for an immediate centralization but one that would take effect when God had given them "rest from all [their] enemies" (Deut 12:10). This condition did not arise until late in David's reign (2 Sam 7:1), and soon after that the temple was constructed. Until that time the law in Exodus 20 was in effect, regulating the building of multiple altars. The laws in Leviticus and Numbers envision the time after the central sanctuary is built.[11]

WHEN ALL IS SAID AND DONE

Two popular understandings of the composition of Genesis, and the Pentateuch as a whole, are clearly wrong when the text is closely examined. On the one hand it is clear that Moses did not write all of the Pentateuch, and on the other it is equally clear that the theory known as the documentary hypothesis is flawed.

The text, however, does claim that Moses played a central role not only in the events that are described in the Pentateuch (the exodus, the law, the wilderness wanderings), but he also had a part in the production of the literary composition known as the Pentateuch, which includes Genesis. Moreover, it is clear that there was editing activity after Moses, and much of the material, particularly in Genesis, shows signs of being previously existing sources.

In other words, it seems best to affirm Moses' central role in the production of Genesis, while ultimately affirming its composite nature. In a recent article on the authorship of the Pentateuch Desmond Alexander, a prolific and insightful thinker on the subject, suggests that some passages provide evidence that the latest editorial work comes from the time of the exile or soon after.[12]

The subject is an important one to examine. Attentive readers will be caught up by material that just doesn't seem to fit into the time period of Moses, and others who have been exposed to theories that deny Mosaic involvement may be too easily persuaded to jettison any connection with that important early Israelite leader. But when it comes down to it, it is both impossible and unnecessary to differentiate Mosaic and non-Mosaic material in any detail. It is impossible because the text isn't interested in signaling to the reader in every case who might be responsible for what. It is unnecessary because in the final analysis the authority of the text is not located in Moses but in God himself. Moses' words aren't canonical; the finished product, the book as it was when the Old Testament canon came to a close, is. Much of the process that led to its completion and also its canonization is lost to us today. By the time the history of its interpretation becomes available to us, the book has assumed its present form. We now join that history by commenting on the finished book of Genesis within the context provided by the Pentateuch and ultimately the whole biblical canon.

PRINCIPLES FOR READING

1. Moses had a foundational connection with the production of the book of Genesis and the Pentateuch as a whole.

2. Moses used sources, presumably oral and written, that were handed down to him from an earlier time.

3. Evidence of significant post-Mosaic redactional activity exists in the book of Genesis and the Pentateuch.

4. It is not possible or useful to definitively and completely divide the pre-Mosaic, Mosaic and post-Mosaic materials from each other.

FOR FURTHER READING

Alexander, T. Desmond. *Abraham in the Negev: A Source-Critical Study of Genesis 20:1-22:19.* Carlisle, U.K.: Paternoster, 1997.

Bloom, Harold, with David Rosenberg. *The Book of J.* New York: Grove Weidenfeld, 1990.

Carr, David M. *Reading the Fractures of Genesis: Historical and Literary Approaches.* Louisville: Westminster John Knox, 1996.

Cassuto, Umberto. *The Documentary Hypothesis.* Translated by I. Abrahams. Jerusalem: Magnes, 1961 (Hebrew ed., 1941).

Garrett, Duane. *Rethinking Genesis: The Sources and Authorship of the First Book of the Bible.* Ross-shire, Scotland: Mentor, 2003.

Kikawada, Isaac M., and Arthur Quinn. *Before Abraham Was: The Unity of Genesis 1-11*. Nashville: Abingdon, 1985.

Kitchen, Kenneth A. *Ancient Orient and Old Testament*. Downers Grove, Ill.: InterVarsity Press, 1967.

Wenham, Gordon J. "Genesis: An Authorship Study and Current Pentateuchal Criticism." *Journal for the Study of the Old Testament* 42 (1988).

Whybray, R. Norman. *The Making of the Pentateuch: A Methodological Study*. JSOTS 53. Sheffield, England: JSOT, 1987.

THREE

THE SHAPE OF
THE BOOK OF GENESIS

Pivotal to understanding any book is an awareness of its literary shape. This shape has three major components: genre, structure and style.

Genre refers to the literary category of a book. A reader's sense of a book's genre determines how to interpret the book. Indeed, we read fiction differently than nonfiction, science differently than mythology and so forth. To misunderstand a genre is to misconstrue its message and meaning.

I use the term *structure* in this chapter simply to refer to a book's outline. What are the main points of a book? Indeed, I would argue that a book can be structured in more than one way. However, the book's outline is not arbitrary, and interpreters must be able to describe a reason for dividing it the way they do.

Finally, *style* refers to the particular way that an author writes. Many definitions of style have been proposed, but we will use this clear and helpful one: "Every writer necessarily makes choices of expression, and it is in these choices, in his 'way of putting things,' that style resides. . . . Every analysis of style . . . is an attempt to find the artistic principles underlying a writer's choice of language."[1]

WHAT TYPE OF BOOK IS GENESIS?

Genre triggers reading strategy. It makes a world of difference whether we identify Genesis in whole or part as history, myth, parable, legend or saga, and all of these categories have been suggested in the history of the interpretation of the book.

Our interest is on the whole book in its present canonical form. It is obvious that within the book of Genesis there is a variety of literary types: genealogy (Gen 5), battle report (Gen 14) and poetic testament (Gen 49), for instance.

In spite of the obvious variety within the book, it is useful to approach genre with the book as a whole in mind. After all, Genesis has a united narrative plot that takes the reader from the creation of the world to the sojourn in Egypt. It recounts past events and does so with a clear chronological structure. The last sentence sounds like a definition of a work of history, and in my opinion such a label makes sense of the generic signals that the reader encounters in the work.

Much of the book, for instance, is recounted using the so-called *vav*-consecutive verbal form that is the basic characteristics of narrative in the Hebrew Bible. Furthermore, the frequent *toledot* formulas (see pp. 46-47, 63) that structure the book also indicate a historical impulse. In addition, there are no dramatic genre shifts between the book of Genesis and the rest of the Pentateuch, and none between the Pentateuch and the so-called historical books that would lead us to read it in any other way than as history. Indeed, if we are speaking of the original intention of the biblical writer(s), the style of the book leaves little space to argue with the obvious conclusion that the author intended Genesis to be read as a work of history that recounts what has taken place in the far-distant past.

Of course, even though the book is intended to be read as representing what actually took place in the past, it is possible that it fails. In other words, it is possible for a book that intends to be historical to fail to accurately represent what took place. Nonetheless, a long tradition of scholarship in both Jewish and Christian circles supports the view that the narrative intends to impart information about events and characters of the far-distant past. Of course, Genesis, like all biblical history writing, may be described as "theological history."

Only in the past century or so have alternative genres for Genesis been seriously proposed.[2] This is the case, for instance, with Hermann Gunkel's belief that Genesis is composed primarily of saga, defined as "a long, prose, traditional narrative having an episodic structure developed around stereotyped themes or objects. . . . The episodes narrate deeds or virtues from the past insofar as they contribute to the composition of the present narrator's words."[3] While this definition is not inherently antagonistic toward a historical intention in the text, it is usually assumed that such sagas "tend to consist of largely unhistorical accretions upon a possibly historical nucleus."[4] Other proposed genre labels for all or part of Genesis include novella, legend, fable, etiology and myth.

Such terms are clearly prejudicial to the historical intentionality of the book. They are motivated more by the modern interpreters' unwillingness and inability to accept the reality of the world of Genesis than by a clear insight into the intention of the text. John Van Seters is an example of a recent critic who affirms the historical intentionality of Genesis (in particular the Yahwist) by means of comparison with Greek historiography. Again, however, this doesn't mean he believes that the events the author narratives actually took place in space and time.

The function of the history contained in Genesis is to provide a prologue and foundation for the nation of Israel and the giving of the law in the book of Exodus. It recounts how God chose Abraham and guided his family as his special people. However, before going on to the structure of the book, we need to discuss the nature of historiography in Genesis.

Theological history. To some people, writing history seems perfectly straightforward. It is a transcript of the past—just the facts. What could be simpler?

However, it is impossible for a human being to present the past as a mere collection of uninterpreted facts, nor would this be desirable even if it were possible. History is different from a videotaped representation of the past in that it involves a historian, one who must interpret these events for a contemporary audience. David Howard has rightly said that

"Only that account is 'history' that attempts to impose some coherence on the past," and "all history writing is of necessity 'perspectival,' even 'subjective,' in the sense that it owes its shape to its author's activity in selecting and communicating material."[5] The subjectivity involved in historical narration does not invalidate the historical intention; rather, the interpreter of a biblical historian must take into account the latter's perspective on the past.

Biblical history does have an antiquarian interest. The author of Genesis believes that God actually created the universe in the past, that Abraham migrated from Mesopotamia to Palestine and that Joseph rose to a high position in Egypt. However, the fact that these events took place is assumed, and not argued. The concern of the text is not to prove the history but rather to impress the reader with the theological significance of these acts. History and theology are closely connected in the biblical text.

All history is ideological; that is, it adopts a perspective through which it tells the story. It interprets events, and does not just record brute facts. Since it is impossible to narrate everything that happens, only those things that are most important to the author and the audience is included, and what is considered important depends on the stance of the author and his or her purpose. But more than selection is involved in writing history; it also includes the relative emphasis that the author puts on various aspects of the history as well as order and application.

Writing history is more like painting, specifically portraiture, than videotaping. V. Philips Long develops this analogy in an intriguing way:

> *Perhaps we can benefit by drawing an analogy between portrait painting, a kind of visual representational art, and historiography, which may fairly be described as verbal representational art. Portrait arts are in a sense "constructionists"; they make creative choices in composing and rendering their historical subject. But they are far from simply imposing structure on an amorphous body of isolated "facts" (an eye here, a nose there). Their task is to observe the contours and the character of their subject, the relationships between the various features, and to capture in a visual representational medium these essentials of their subject. No two portraits are exactly alike, of course, because no two portrait artists see the subject in just the same way or make the same*

creative choices in rendering it. But neither are competent portraits of the same subject utterly unlike, for they are constrained by the facts—the contours and structures of the subject. In their representational craft, portrait artists compose (i.e., construct) their painting, but they do not simply impose structure on their subject. Might it be the same for narrative historians?[6]

In conclusion, it is possible, even necessary, both to affirm the historical intention of a text like Genesis as well as to search for the theological motivation behind its particular shaping of the past events.

THE STRUCTURE OF THE BOOK OF GENESIS

Determining the structure of a book is a way of seeing its outline and describing how the author has shaped its contents. In the case of a narrative book like Genesis, the structure helps the reader see the flow and dynamics of the plot. It's possible to describe the structure in more than one way, depending on what narrative clues the reader is paying attention. In the case of Genesis, two structures are both interesting and illuminating.

One fascinating structure can be easily missed by the reader who reads the book in English. That is because the key Hebrew word *toledot* is often translated by more than one English phrase in most translations. The complete Hebrew phrase is *'elleh toledot,* which occurs eleven times in the book of Genesis (2:4; 5:1; 6:9; 10:1; 11:10; 11:27; 25:12; 25:19; 36:1 [36:9]; 37:2), has been translated in a number of different ways, including "these are the generations," "this is the family history," "this is the history of the descendants" and "this is the account." The phrase is typically followed by a personal name with the exception of Genesis 2:4, which names instead the "heavens and the earth." Following this first occurrence, the narrative divides into the following sections: "these are the generations of" Adam, Noah, Noah's sons, Shem, Terah, Ishmael, Isaac, Esau (the formula is given twice for Esau, 36:1, 9) and Jacob. Thus the book of Genesis has a prologue (1:1—2:3) followed by ten episodes. The person named is not necessarily the main character, but the beginning point of the section that also closes with his death. This device, accordingly, provides a sense of unity to the book as well as a notion of generational progression.

A second approach to the structure of Genesis considers the book's transitions in terms of content and style, which is very noticeable to readers of the English text. First, it is possible to divide the book into two subsections: Genesis 1:1—11:26 and 11:27—50:26. The former is the "primeval history" and covers the time between creation and the tower of Babel. These chapters cover an indeterminably long period of time in the far-distance past. The second part is characterized by a slowing down of the plot and a focus on one man, Abraham, and his family for four generations. These chapters are often called the "patriarchal narratives"; they follow the movements of the people of promise from Abraham's call in Genesis 12:1 to the death of Joseph at the end of the book. Both of these divisions of Genesis begin with a creation initiated by the power of God. In Genesis 1:1 God calls the universe into existence by the power of his word; in Genesis 12:1 God calls a special people into existence by the power of his word.[7]

A further subdivision can be made within the second part of Genesis between the patriarchal narratives and the Joseph story. The former are episodic, short accounts of the events in the lives of Abraham, Isaac and Jacob. The Joseph story (Genesis 37; 39—50) is a connected plot that recounts how Abraham's family came to live Egypt. The story continues in the book of Exodus. The Joseph story provides the transition between a family of seventy to seventy-five people that went into Egypt and a nation that, four hundred years later, is poised on the edge of the exodus.

In my presentation of the interpretation of the book (see chapters 7-9), I will utilize a simple three-part structure for Genesis:

• The Primeval History: Genesis 1—11

• The Patriarchal Narratives: Genesis 12—36

• The Joseph Story: Genesis 37—50

THE LITERARY STYLE OF GENESIS

The literary style of biblical books reached a new point of interest beginning in the 1980s. The study of biblical literature as literature was not a totally new idea, but it was put on a back burner for about two centuries because scholars thought it was more important to discuss the issue of the history of composition of the books rather than their literary quality.[8] Regarding Genesis specifically, scholars were fascinated by the issue of sources (J, E, D, P) rather than in the questions of the shape of the book as it now stands. Indeed, the two impulses work against each other. That is, dissecting a book by its sources discourages readings that look at plot development or characterization.

Many books and articles have been written in just the last twenty years plumbing the literary qualities of Genesis.[9] The results have been fascinating and extensive, too much so to be represented here fully. I will simply give an example of the type of study that discerns the literary style of Genesis, and then I will implement my literary sensitivities as I present my interpretation of the book in chapters seven through nine.

In terms of literary study, genre and structure are first and foremost. In a narrative text like Genesis, we also need to understand the story's plot. The plot is presented by a narrator, and the narration strategy chosen by the author is informative. Genesis is similar to the vast majority of biblical texts in being narrated not by a character or a specific individual, but rather by a third-person, omniscient narrator, who knows what people are thinking and doing (even when they are alone), and is even able to disclose divine motivation. The voice of the narrator is often the authoritative guide in the story, directing the reader in his or her analysis and response to the events and characters of the story. It has been pointed out that readers react to a third-person narrator with an unconscious submissiveness. David Rhoads and Donald Michie note, "When the narrator is omniscient and invisible, readers tend to be unaware of the narrator's biases, values, and conceptual view of the word."[10] The narrator adopts a certain point of view that shapes the readers responses to the events of the story.

The narrator is also the one who introduces the reader to the characters of the story. Selectivity and interpretation are involved in the presentation of character. One common trait of biblical narration is its reticence to discuss motivation or physical description. The story mostly moves along by showing rather than telling, and the showing is often done through the presentation of direct discourse. For instance, in chapter 8 we will see that Abraham is presented in a way that makes his journey of faith the central concern. Not all matters of his life are of interest, and so only those that show his response to the covenant promises in Genesis 12:1-3 are highlighted.

Because Hebrew narrative is restrained rather than wordy, the words used are typically pregnant with significance. This demands that the reader pays close attention to the details of the story: significance may be found in a single descriptive word or even the lack of a word where one might be expected.

For instance, in Bruce Waltke's illuminating study of the Cain and Abel story (Gen 4), he applies some of these insights to the question, Why didn't God accept Cain's sacrifice.[11] Was Cain's sacrifice unacceptable because it was not a bloody sacrifice? Or was it rejected because it was not offered in faith? The enigma of Cain's sacrifice has arisen because of the silence of the Old Testament text concerning Cain's motives for bringing his sacrifice and God's motives for rejecting it. The text introduces Cain and Abel very abruptly and tells only briefly the story leading up to Abel's murder.

Waltke points to indirect indications within the text that help solve the problem. Generally speaking, the passage becomes clearer once it is realized that the text contrasts Cain and Abel's actions. Waltke here follows Robert Alter, mentioned earlier, who highlights character contrast as a favorite device of Hebrew narrative. Waltke notices two important differences in terms of the sacrifice that each brother brought. The narrator mentions that Abel brought the "firstborn" of the flock, whereas Cain's sacrifice is not qualified in any equivalent way. Waltke's conclusion seems warranted: "Abel's sacrifice is characterized as the best of its class and . . . Cain's is not. The point seems to be that Abel's sacrifice represents heartfelt worship; Cain's represents unacceptable tokenism."[12]

PRINCIPLES FOR READING

The following principles are taken from chapters two and three.

1. Determine what the text indicates concerning its history of composition. How did Genesis reach its final form?

2. No matter what conclusion is reached in answer to the first point, the interpreter should treat the final form of the text as a whole.

3. Identify the genre of the book.

4. Determine the structure of the book.

5. Be sensitive to the literary style of the book.

FOR FURTHER READING

Alter, Robert. *The Art of Biblical Narrative*. New York: Basic Books, 1981.

Berlin, Adele. *A Poetics and Interpretation of Biblical Narrative*. Sheffield, England: Almond, 1983.

Borgman, Paul. *Genesis: The Story We Haven't Heard*. Downers Grove, Ill.: InterVarsity Press, 2001.

Fokkelman, J. P. *Narrative Art in Genesis*. Amsterdam: Van Gorcum, 1975.

Longman, Tremper, III. *Literary Approaches to Biblical Interpretation*. Grand Rapids: Zondervan, 1987.

Sternberg, Meir. *The Poetics of Biblical Narrative*. Bloomington: Indiana University Press, 1985.

PART

READING GENESIS
IN ITS OWN WORLD

■   ■   ■

In the United States many have grown up with the Bible in their home—even if their families were not particularly religious. The stories of Genesis are among the best known from Scripture among church people as well as in the general population. In particular, most people are familiar with the biblical account of creation as taking place in six days with a seventh day of rest. They are familiar with the stories of the creation of Adam and Eve. Furthermore, people are aware that the Bible describes a devastating flood and most people could probably name Noah as the hero of the day.

However, most people today are unaware of the rival creation texts and flood stories of ancient Israel's neighbors. But the ancient writers and readers of Scripture knew them well. And they likely understood the biblical stories against the background of these texts.

Thanks to modern archaeology and the deciphering of ancient languages, we now have the opportunity of gaining an intimate acquaintance with these texts. Knowledge of these ancient texts is a guard against reading modern scientific perspectives and questions back into Genesis. They also help us recover the ancient worldview of those who lived in biblical times.

While space does not permit an exhaustive treatment, our look at creation and the flood in the light of the ancient Near East will illustrate some broader principles for interpreting the Old Testament. And the biblical creation and flood narratives aren't the only stories that have an ancient Near Eastern background. Further knowledge of ancient Near Eastern backgrounds may be found in good commentaries as well as in some of the books listed at the end of the chapter six.

FOUR

MYTH OR HISTORY?

Genesis and the Enuma Elish

Genesis was not written in a vacuum. It may be the oldest part of Scripture, but it is not, by far, the oldest literature from the ancient Near East.

The earliest literatures that bear on the study of the Bible come from ancient Mesopotamia and Egypt, the two cultural powerhouses of the day. At the earliest, Moses should be dated to the fifteenth century B.C., while the first pieces of Sumerian and Egyptian literature come from the first part of the third millennium. Also significant for the study of the Old Testament is the literature, particularly that written in Ugaritic, from Israel's nearest neighbors, literature that reflects Canaanite religious ideas.

Chapters four and five explore different aspects of the abundant ancient Near Eastern literature that shows similarity to parts of the book of Genesis. The cultural background of any biblical book is important, but for Genesis it is particularly crucial considering the literature that has survived. In this chapter, we will read the account of creation in the light of rival accounts from the surrounding nations. In the process the question arises whether the Genesis creation account is rightly considered myth or history. In addition, we will evaluate the existence of flood stories similar to the biblical account of Noah. In chapter five, the significance of the description of customs similar to those observed by the patriarchs will be evaluated.

ANCIENT NEAR EASTERN CREATION ACCOUNTS

Today as I read Genesis 1—2 my thoughts go to high school biology and physics. How does the biblical depiction of creation relate to the big bang theory and evolution?

No doubt, Genesis 1—2 has bearing on our evaluation of these modern scientific accounts of cosmic and human origins. But a moment's thought will jar us into remembering that this comparison would not have occurred to ancient authors and readers. It is certain that the biblical account of creation was not written to counter Charles Darwin or Stephen Hawking, but it was written in the light of rival descriptions of creation. And thanks to the discoveries of archaeologists and language experts over the past couple of centuries, we have in hand at least some of those ideas that would have competed for the hearts and minds of ancient Israelites. Rather than providing an exhaustive list of the many different myths of Israel's neighbors, I will cite points of comparison and contrast between the biblical accounts on the one side and those of the Egyptians, Mesopotamians and Canaanites on the other.

From the time of the patriarchs down through the rest of the period of the Old Testament, the children of Abraham lived in the midst of a pagan world. Only Israel worshiped Yahweh, while the rest of the nations had their own gods and goddesses—and they also had their own creation accounts. Since God's people were constantly tempted to worship the deities of other nations, we shouldn't be surprised that the biblical accounts of creation were shaped in such a way as to provide a clear distinction from those of other nations. Even so, there are similarities. In any case, the most interesting and the richest reading of the biblical creation accounts takes place in the light of the rival accounts of the ancient Near East. However, before making the comparison, we will need to briefly describe a few of the leading creation accounts from the ancient Near East.

Egypt. Throughout its history, and particularly at the time of Moses, Israel had contact with the Egyptians. The biblical tradition states that the

Israelites left Egypt under the leadership of Moses, who himself was raised and presumably educated in Pharaoh's own household. For this reason, it's reasonable that Egyptian ideas about creation were known from the earliest point of Israel's history as a nation.

Surprisingly, we have very few continuous mythic narratives in Egyptian.[1] Egyptian creation ideas are found primarily in magical texts, particularly on texts written on coffins and the walls of pyramids, though there is the exception of the Shabaka Stone, which preserves what is known as the Memphite Theology. While there are many similarities between the different descriptions of creation to be found in Egyptian texts, there are also a variety of metaphors that are employed.[2] Acts of creation are also attributed to various deities. Different cult centers in Egypt (Memphis, Hermopolis, Heliopolis) had their own version of creation, though we can also observe some attempts at synthesis.

The basic cosmology of the Egyptians seems somewhat constant. The primeval waters are called Nun and it is out of the waters that creation emerged. One prominent idea was that the creator god, sometimes Atum and other times Amon-Re, emerged from the waters through an act of self-creation, and through him developed the other gods and goddesses who represent the various parts and forces of nature.[3] The form of the emergence from Nun was the primeval mound, perhaps mythically reflecting the fertile soil that was the source of life left after the annual Nile floodwaters receded.

Egyptian religion was never a single idea but rather an amalgamation and association of loosely associated religious concepts derived from a variety of cult centers. Thus we shouldn't be surprised that at Memphis, one of those cult centers, there was a rival creation myth surrounding the god Ptah. The best-known expression of this myth is from the so-called Memphite Theology, also known as the Shabaka Stone.[4] The latter name comes from the fact that the text is preserved on a stone that was inscribed at the time of the Nubian pharaoh Shabaqo (716-702 B.C.), though scholars are agreed that the composition comes from a much earlier time. In this account Ptah amalgamated with Ta-tenen, the god who represents the primeval hillock and then engenders the sun god. In this way the main deity

of Memphis, Ptah, displaces the god Atum as the creator. What is interesting to us, however, is the different process of creation used by Ptah.
Rather than by sneezing or masturbating, Ptah creates the world by the
words of his mouth: "So were all the gods born, Atum and his Ennead as
well, for it is through what the heart plans and the tongue commands that
every divine speech has evolved."[5]

There is scant reference or allusion to the creation of humanity in
Egyptian literature. What information we do have is that humans were
created from the tears of the god of the sun, an etiology that may be based
on the similarity of the words *weep, people* and *tears.*

Mesopotamia. The earliest literature in the region of Mesopotamia, indeed, the earliest literature known, comes from ancient Sumer. And
though the Sumerians left behind an extensive creation literature, we
will bypass a presentation of these creation ideas in favor of focusing on
two creation texts from Akkadian literature. Akkadian was the language
of the Babylonians and Assyrians. The latter were the heirs to Sumerian
ideas and are contemporary with the Israelites during the Old Testament
time period.

The most significant creation text written in Akkadian gets its name
from its first words "when on high," which in Akkadian is *Enuma Elish.*
Even though creation is an essential element of the myth, the ultimate
purpose of the composition was to proclaim the exaltation of Marduk to
the head of the pantheon. Most scholars today would associate the exaltation of Marduk and the composition of this text to the reign of Nebuchadnezzar I (twelfth century B.C.).

The text begins with a theogony, that is, a record of the birth and generations of the gods and goddesses.[6] The oldest deities were Apsu and
Tiamat, the waters under the earth and of the sea respectively, whose
mingling waters produced the next generations of the gods and goddesses. Soon there was a generation gap with which to deal. Father Apsu
grew tired of his noisy children, and, against the wishes of his wife, determined to kill his divine offspring. The latter, however, heard of the
plot, and Ea, the god of wisdom, recited a magic spell and killed Apsu
before he could act.

While Ea's actions were effective in the short term, they also served to enrage Tiamat, a more formidable foe than Apsu. Not even Ea could hope to subdue Tiamat. All looked helpless until Marduk, the offspring of Ea and Damkina, stepped forward to assume the role of hero. However, he did not volunteer without imposing conditions. He demanded and received the kingship of the gods, and with that status he set out to meet Tiamat in combat.

In the meantime Tiamat had appointed Qingu to be the leader of her forces, apparently as her consort in place of Apsu. It was against the combined forces of chaos that Marduk ultimately waged war.

The battle between Marduk and Tiamat is vividly described. At the climax of the conflict, Marduk let loose a wind that distended her body, shooting an arrow into her mouth that tore her belly and extinguished her life. With the death of Tiamat, her supporting army, led by Qingu, dispersed in disarray. Tiamat had given Qingu the tablets of destiny, showing his sovereignty, but Marduk took them from him and kept them, ultimately handing them over to Anu, the god of heaven.

Marduk then turned his attention to the body of Tiamat, which he split into two parts, "like a fish for drying."[7] With one half, he fashioned the heavens, and with the other the earth. Using the heavenly bodies, Marduk also ordered time. After this, Marduk decided to make human beings:

> *I shall compact blood, I shall cause bones to be,*
> *I shall make stand a human being, let "Man" be its name.*
> *I shall create humankind,*
> *They shall bear the gods' burden that those may rest.*

Marduk then executed Qingu, the demon-god, for his crimes, and from his blood made humanity. After this, the gods honored Marduk by constructing the city of Babylon and Marduk's temple-home Esagila. The *Enuma Elish* concludes with the gods proclaiming Marduk's glory by pronouncing his fifty names.

A second Akkadian text, *Atrahasis,* is named after its leading character and presents an alternative account of the creation of humanity.[8] The first scene opens at a time when only the gods exist. Conflict arises though when the lower gods go on strike against the more powerful gods, represented by Enlil. The former had been digging irrigation canals and are tired of their work. They picket Enlil's residence with the result that that great god determines to create alternative workers. Belet-ili, the birth goddess, is then directed to build the first humans to "bear the yoke, the task of Enlil. Let man assume the drudgery of the gods."[9] To accomplish this task, Belit-ili with the help of the wise god Enki, killed one of the lesser gods, We-ila, and mixed his blood with clay, thus producing humanity.

Canaan. Throughout the biblical period, Israelites were tempted to worship the gods and goddesses of the former inhabitants of the land, the Canaanites. While David succeeded in removing all significant representatives of these people from Palestine, their relatives persisted to the north in what is today Lebanon and Syria. The most active of the deities of Canaan are the well known Baal, El, Asherah and Anat. Since Canaanite religion had such a strong pull on the hearts of Israel, it's particularly important to examine its concepts of creation.

Actually, no creation text has been discovered among the tablets found at ancient Ugarit, the main source of our knowledge of Canaanite literature and religion. Nevertheless, a broken episode of the famous "Baal Cycle" may have originally contained such a narrative, since the extant part bears a formal similarity to the *Enuma Elish* in that it involves a conflict between the chief god of the pantheon (here Baal) and a sea god(dess) (here Yam). In the Ugaritic text we learn that Yam attempts to assume the kingship of the pantheon and demands Baal as his prisoner. Baal resists and commissions the craftsman god Kothar-wa-Hasis to make two clubs for him. With these clubs, Baal battles, defeats and drinks Yam. At this point the text is broken, but many scholars believe that what followed the defeat of the Sea (Yam) was a creation account on analogy with the *Enuma Elish*.[10]

COMPETING ACCOUNTS OF CREATION

How does knowledge of other ancient Near Eastern creation texts influence our interpretation of Genesis 1—2? To answer this question, we will want to pay attention to both the similarities and differences between the

Hebrew and broader Near Eastern accounts.[11] A fuller presentation of the picture of the Genesis creation account awaits a later chapter. Here I will be selective, guided by textual data of the Near East.

There are certain general as well as particular similarities between Genesis 1—2 and other creation texts. A few key examples will illustrate.

First, it is interesting to note that most accounts presume a period of chaos followed by order. In addition, the primordial chaos is pictured as a watery mass. The *Enuma Elish* describes how Marduk created the cosmos out of the body of Tiamat (the sea), the Baal myth presumably follows this pattern with Baal creating the world from Yam (also the sea), while the Egyptian myths see the primeval hillock emanating from Nun, the primeval waters.

Genesis 1 also describes the initial material of the earth as "formless and empty, and darkness covered the deep waters," and on the second day the appearance of land results from the separation of the "waters of the heavens from the waters of the earth" (Gen 1:6). Thus there seems to be a similarity in the conception of creation from an undifferentiated mass.

As an example of a particular connection, we should take note of the Memphite Theology (see pp. 73-74). In Genesis 1 God speaks to accomplish the different acts of creation. In the Memphite Theology the word of Ptah brings created things into existence.

But perhaps more significantly, there appears to be an increasing similarity in certain conceptions of the creation of humanity. But here we detect difference as well.

Mesopotamian texts provide a close echo of the biblical account of human creation. *Enuma Elish* narrates how Marduk slaughtered the demon god Qingu and took his blood and mixed it with the clay. *Atrahasis* describes the slaughter of the god We-ila and how Belit-ili mixes his blood with clay. Finally, the gods spit on the concoction and humanity is brought into being. *Atrahasis* in particular makes it very clear that humans are created for a purpose. They are to perform manual labor to replace the lesser deities who had gone on strike.

The biblical account of creation also speaks of humans coming into existence by the combination of elements. Adam is created from the dust of the ground and the breath of God, probably indicating the human connection with the created order and their special relationship with the deity. Eve is later created from Adam's rib. One scholar has found significance in the text's use of *rib* in the fact that the Sumerian words for *life* and *rib* sound similar *(ti[l])*,[12] though this seems far-fetched.

The Genesis creation texts treat humanity with considerably more respect than their Mesopotamia counterparts. To be sure, Adam and Eve are created for manual labor, to tend the garden, but they are also described as created in the image of God, and the relationship with their God seems to be more personal.[13] Here we can see how an examination of the ancient Near Eastern literature illuminates the Genesis account and the intention of the biblical author.

Even so, on one issue the similarity still leaves us with questions. Did the creation of Adam literally take place the way it is narrated, or is the story of Adam's creation shaped to teach us things about the nature of humanity? Did God really use the dust of the ground to form Adam's body and blow his breath into it? If so, then we should probably see the Mesopotamian account as a perversion of a fundamental truth preserved accurately in the biblical tradition.

More likely, however, is the idea that Genesis has taken the Near Eastern tradition and then substituted God's breath for either divine spit or blood. This communicates both the truth that humans are creatures connected to the earth and beings who have a special relationship with God, for it was God who created humanity.

DIFFERENCES BETWEEN GENESIS AND OTHER CREATION ACCOUNTS

However, even more impressive than the similarities are the differences the Genesis account has with the broader ancient Near Eastern creation tradition. In the first place, notice a major difference in the creation process: the lack of conflict in Genesis.

In particular, the Mesopotamian and the Canaanite accounts of creation feature conflict at the center of the creation. Marduk defeats the forces of chaos (Tiamat), as does Baal (Yam). In spite of tremendous efforts to find traces of a conflict myth, no Yahweh faces no such rival in the Genesis account.[14] God shapes the watery mass into a beautifully ordered world over the course of the six days of creation.[15]

Of course, this highlights the most important and fundamental difference between Genesis and all the creation accounts, and it underlines the single most important theme of these chapters: Yahweh created the cosmos! Marduk didn't do it, nor did Baal, Atum, Re or any other god. Of course there was no conflict at the time of creation because there was no rival who could stand against Yahweh. The purpose of the creation texts, when read in the light of alternative contemporary accounts, was to assert the truth about who was responsible.

SUMMARY

Reading Genesis 1—2 in the light of Egyptian, Mesopotamian and Canaanite creation accounts enriches our understanding of the former, mainly through contrast. The main contrast has to do with the identity and nature of the Creator. The biblical account presents one God, who alone is God, who created the world. This one God created unopposed. But in the Mesopotamian and related Canaanite accounts the cosmos came into existence by means of conflict. According to Genesis, conflict is introduced into the world not by the gods but by humanity's rebellion (Gen 3).

The difference in the conception of the divine realm also explains why there is a contrast between the presence or lack of a theogony, or account of the birth of the gods. In addition and related to this is the fact that many of the aspects of creation that were thought to be divine in the ancient Near Eastern are said to be created in the biblical account. In Egypt, for instance, the main god and creator is, in most accounts, the sun, whether given the name Amun or Aten or Re. According to the Bible, Yahweh created the sun on the fourth day along with the other heavenly bodies.

Perhaps most dramatically, we should read the account of the creation of humanity in the light of Mesopotamian conceptions. In the *Enuma Elish*, humans are a union of the clay and the blood of a demon god; in the Bible a union of dust and the breath of God. Certainly this is not an accident but is likely an intentional polemic on the part of the biblical author. On the surface of it the biblical account is noble and dignified in a way that the ancient Near Eastern account is not. It is also true that in both traditions the divine realm puts humans to work, but the cultivation of the Garden is nobler work than the digging of irrigation ditches, particularly after hearing the complaints of the lesser gods who, according to *Atrahasis*, had that duty beforehand.

(Interpretive principles and further reading for chapter four can be found at the end of chapter six [pp. 97-98].)

FIVE

Noah and Utnapishtim

Whose Flood Story Should We Trust?

A story, perhaps apocryphal, relates the excitement of discovery by one of the great pioneers in the study of Mesopotamian literature, the otherwise staid Englishman George Adam Smith. The setting is the late nineteenth century, when thousands of clay tablets from Mesopotamia had been added to the collection of the British Museum. As Smith was doing preliminary readings of these tablets, he became the first person since antiquity to read the eleventh tablet of the Gilgamesh Epic. This is the part that tells of the great flood. As the story goes, when Smith read the tablet and saw its incredible similarity to the biblical account of the flood, he climbed on top of a library table and started ripping off his clothes in his excitement![1]

Whether or not this story is true, it certainly reflects the reality of the excitement scholars felt when they saw the close connection between the various ancient flood traditions. In a word, they felt that they had found the origin of the biblical story. It was simply a rewrite of the ancient Near Eastern account! Frederick Delitzsch, the son of the great Lutheran commentator Franz Delitzsch and a powerful force in the relatively new discipline of the study of ancient Mesopotamia (Assyriology), as well as other scholars argued that the Bible was essentially a poor reflection of these great ancient myths and legends.[2] But is this the only explanation? Before we can answer that question, we need to introduce in more detail precisely what ancient extrabiblical literature says about the flood.

MESOPOTAMIAN STORIES OF THE FLOOD

Ancient Mesopotamia (Sumerian and Akkadian traditions combined) has left us three major accounts of the flood (Eridu Genesis, Gilgamesh and *Atrahasis*), plus other texts that mention the flood (e.g., the Sumerian King List). In other words, it appears that the flood was a well-attested tradition in ancient Mesopotamia. Besides the fact that the flood hero (the equivalent of Noah in the biblical text) had a different name in these compositions (Ziusudra, Utnapishtim and Atrahasis), the basic story remains the same,[3] though the fullest account comes in the Gilgamesh Epic. For our purposes we will focus only on the Gilgamesh Epic since it provides the clearest parallel with the biblical account.

The Gilgamesh Epic. Surely the best known of ancient Mesopotamian compositions, the Gilgamesh Epic contains no creation story, but its flood story is the one with the most relevant similarities to the biblical flood story. However, Gilgamesh only narrates the flood in the context of a larger plot, which I will recount here only in summary form.

Gilgamesh is the king of Uruk, and at the beginning of the tale he is quite unpopular with his subjects.[4] As a result, they turn to the god Anu with their complaint, and he responds by creating Enkidu, who would presumably be Gilgamesh's rival and perhaps distract him from his oppressive behavior toward the citizens of Uruk. At first, however, Enkidu didn't enter the city of Uruk. He is a primeval man and finds the company of animals in the countryside more to his keeping. This, of course, doesn't serve the interests of the people, so they send a prostitute out of the city to "civilize" him.

The prostitute successfully seduces Enkidu, whose company is no longer appreciated by the animals, so he reluctantly goes with her to Uruk. Once there, Enkidu meets Gilgamesh, and they fight. Through their struggle, they become fast friends and embark on a series of exploits together.

Among other adventures, they defeat Huwawa, the protector of the cedar forest of Lebanon. During this time, Gilgamesh's prowess and beauty attract the goddess Ishtar, who propositions him. Gilgamesh, knowing the fates of her previous lovers, rejects her, which causes her to run to her father, Anu, for revenge. Anu doesn't want to kill Gilgamesh, but instead punishes him by striking down Enkidu.

Gilgamesh is greatly moved by the death of Enkidu, not only because he is his friend but also, it appears, because Enkidu's death confronts him with his own mortality. The rest of the tale is the story of Gilgamesh's search for an answer to death.

It is this question that brings him to Utnapishtim, since Utnapishtim is the only human not to experience death. Gilgamesh's question to Utnapishtim as to why he has not died is what leads the latter to recount his experience with the flood (tablet 11 of the Epic).

In answer to Gilgamesh, Utnapishtim recounts the time the gods decided to bring a flood against humanity. Ea, however, communicated with one of his devotees and told him to build a ship that would carry its inhabitants through the ravages of the flood. The dimensions of this ark were that of a great cube. Upon completing the ark in only seven days, Utnapishtim loaded the boat with provisions, but more importantly he also loaded his family and animals. When all were safely within the ship, the horrifying rains began. Even the gods were "frightened by the deluge." The storm lasted for seven days, and the ship came to a standstill on Mount Nimush. Utnapishtim at that point let out a series of birds—two doves followed by a swallow—to see if dry land was yet exposed. The last bird did the trick, and they disembarked. Their first action was to offer a sacrifice, which was a great delight to the gods, who were hungry from the lack of human attention. Enlil, however, was none too pleased, and he indicted Ea for his lack of loyalty to his fellow deities. Even so, Ea was able to calm Enlil down, and the latter then determined to confer immortality on Utnapishtim and his wife. The story is fascinating but depressing to Gilgamesh because he has now learned that Utnapishtim's immortality is unrepeatable. Gilgamesh himself will not find the answer to his dilemma in this way.

However, he is not convinced that the place itself does not preserve him from death until he finds that he can't even avoid its distant cousin, sleep. He falls asleep and this convinces him that death is not far away.

Nonetheless, on his way home, Gilgamesh is informed by Utnapishtim about a plant at the bottom of the water, which seems to have the power to preserve life. Though Gilgamesh successfully retrieves the plant, a serpent steals it from him. (This episode is likely an explanation of why snakes seem to renew their life through the shedding of their skin.) At the end of the story Gilgamesh has come to terms with the fact that he will not live forever, except in his great acts.[5]

Connections to Genesis 6—9. We can't deny the similarities between the Gilgamesh Epic and the biblical flood story. On the other hand, clear differences emerge when we compare the stories. We will treat both as we now follow the plot of the biblical account.

Like Enlil, Yahweh determines to use a catastrophic flood to bring judgment on his human creatures. However, what motivates them is importantly different. Enlil was tired of the "noise" of humanity, probably as a result of overpopulation. The biblical account is set in the framework of the creation of humanity, which encouraged the multiplication of the human race (Gen 1:28). And the biblical motivation for the flood was moral rather than a matter of divine inconvenience. The biblical flood story begins with the statement that "the LORD observed the extent of human wickedness on the earth, and he saw that everything they thought or imagined was consistently and totally evil" (Gen 6:5). The moral dimension of the flood story is missing from the Mesopotamian rendition. Indeed, if anything, we might almost say that the Gilgamesh Epic depicts Enlil and the gods as doing something wrong and paying the consequences.

The choice of the "flood hero" also underlines a significant difference between the accounts. In Mesopotamia, the god of wisdom goes underground and secretly alerts his follower of the coming deluge. In the biblical account, Yahweh, the God who brings the flood, is also the God who assures the continuance of the human race after the flood by alerting Noah, who was a "righteous man" (Gen 6:9).

In a number of points in the story there are differences in the midst of the similarities. Both stories record the building of the boat, the length of the flood, the bringing of animals and other humans on the boat, but the details are different.

To illustrate an episode that is similar yet vastly different, we can compare the two accounts of the offering of sacrifices. The similarity is that in both cases the flood hero offers sacrifices to their God or gods as the first act after disembarking. However, the depiction of the reaction of the gods in the Mesopotamian account is radically different from the biblical account. After all, Mesopotamian gods depended on human sacrifice as a form of nourishment. In a word, the gods are starved because of the destruction of humanity, so after the altar fires are lit, the Epic says:

> *The gods smelled the savor,*
> *The gods smelled the sweet savor,*
> *The gods crowded around the sacrificer like flies.* [6]

Perhaps the most striking similarity between the two accounts is the use of birds to determine whether or not the floodwaters have receded. According to the biblical text:

> *Noah opened the window he had made in the boat and released a raven. The bird flew back and forth until the floodwaters on the earth had dried up. He also released a dove to see if the water had receded and it could find dry ground. But the dove could find no place to land because the water still covered the ground. So it returned to the boat, and Noah held out his hand and drew the dove back inside. After waiting another seven days, Noah released the dove again. This time the dove returned to him in the evening with a fresh olive leaf in its beak. Then Noah knew that the floodwaters were almost gone. He waited another seven days and then released the dove again. This time it did not come back. (Gen 8:6-12)*

In the Gilgamesh Epic the ark has come to rest on Mount Nimush, and after six days pass we hear the following report:

> *When the seventh day arrived,*
> *I released a dove to go free,*
> *The dove went and returned,*
> *No landing place came to view, it turned back.*

I released a swallow to go free,
The swallow went and returned,
No landing place came to view, it turned back.
I sent a raven to go free,
The raven went forth, saw the ebbing of the waters,
It ate, circled, left droppings, did not turn back.

While the order of birds is different in each account (raven, dove; dove, dove; swallow, raven), the similarity of this episode cannot be explained as chance or common ancient cultural custom. We will have to seek another explanation, and it is to that we now turn.

RELATIONSHIPS BETWEEN THE ANCIENT NEAR EASTERN ACCOUNTS AND GENESIS

How can we best understand the relationship between the flood stories of the ancient Near East, particularly in regard to the Genesis account? Though there are differences, the similarities are close enough that they can't be disregarded, but are they so close that the only explanation is that Genesis simply borrowed and adapted a myth from ancient Mesopotamia?

First, we must make an admission, one that should be made by everyone who addresses this question. We can't be dogmatic in our assessment of the relationship between these texts. In other words, we can't prove our interpretation of the matter beyond all doubt. Indeed, how we construe the relationship is shaped to a large extent by our presuppositions. There are limits on how we might understand it, and certain interpretations are ruled out or rendered improbable by the nature of our knowledge. For instance, it is highly unlikely that the Gilgamesh Epic borrowed from the written account of the flood in the Bible. In the first place, the Mesopotamian tradition has its roots in Mesopotamian literature long before the written account in Genesis. Furthermore, rarely does an advanced culture borrow from an inferior culture. It is more likely that Podunk City would be influenced culturally by New York City than vice versa, and in the ancient world Israel was Podunk City and Babylon was New York City.

However, there are more options than simply concluding that the Bible borrowed from Babylon. An equally plausible explanation is that both traditions go back to a real event. At this point I will avoid the question of the nature of the flood, that is, whether the flood was an exceptionally large local flood or a global one. Whatever the case, the flood etched itself in the memory of the survivors. The story of the flood and its interpretation would have been passed down from generation to generation. Looking at the situation from the perspective of the Bible's view of humanity, the following hypothetical reconstruction is possible.

After the flood, humanity descended from Noah and his family in the way that earlier humanity descended from Adam. Like Adam's descendants, Noah's eventually split into two communities, one that followed God and one that rejected God. The latter adopted its own religious perspective, that of polytheistic idolatry. The flood story continued to be transmitted from generation to generation, but its explanation was changed to conform to the new religious perspective. The Gilgamesh Epic and the other ancient Near Eastern flood traditions was representative of the tradition that remembered the flood through the lens of a polytheistic religious system, while the Genesis account is a later written form of the interpretation of those who worshiped Yahweh.

Whether a person accepts one or the other account, or none at all, is a matter of his or her religious perspective, including an assessment of the nature of biblical authority. That any particular model of understanding the similarities and differences between the biblical and Mesopotamian tradition can be proved is not likely. However, this discussion demonstrates that the position that Israel simply borrowed the Mesopotamian story and adapted it to its own viewpoint is not the only possible conclusion.

The perspective adopted in this chapter benefits our understanding of the story. If we study the biblical account in the light of the Mesopotamian account, the contrast between the respective deities is thrown into sharp relief. While Yahweh reveals himself as a God who judges sin, he is not like the capricious deity Enlil. In the context of judgment we find grace in the biblical account; this is missing in the ancient Near Eastern account.

[Interpretive principles and further reading for chapter five can be found at the end of chapter six (see pp. 97-98).]

SIX

ABRAHAM AND NUZI

Patriarchal Customs in Their Cultural Context

In chapters four and five we examined the similarities and differences between ancient creation and flood stories. For our final look at the ancient Near Eastern background of Genesis, we take up a somewhat different subject, namely, how the cultural customs we observe in Genesis compare with those in other regions of the ancient Near East. The burning question here is whether or not the patriarchs fit into the time period the Bible situates them. Another benefit of this comparative study is that it further illuminates biblical customs that seem so strange to us.

CAN WE DATE ABRAHAM?

Is it possible to place Abraham on a time line? For that matter, can we give any biblical event an absolute date as opposed to a relative date? A relative date is one given to an event relative to other events. All the dates that are given in the Bible are relative to other events. As an example, let's consider the date of the exodus from Egypt. Perhaps the most important chronological evidence for the date of the exodus is found in 1 Kings 6:1:

> *It was mid-spring, during the fourth year of Solomon's reign, that he began the construction of the Temple of the LORD. This was 480 years after the people of Israel were delivered from their slavery in the land of Egypt.*

This type of relative dating certainly helps us envision the chronological relationship between biblical events, but it doesn't allow us to put it on our dateline; that is, it doesn't allow us to give it an absolute date.

An absolute date allows us to see just how long ago from today an event took place. There is more than one way to keep a calendar, but most of us are familiar with an absolute dating system that uses as a fixed point the birth of Jesus Christ. The year I am writing this book is A.D. 2004.[1] And, as is well known, dates before Christ's birth are counted backward and cited as B.C. ("before Christ"). Recently, objections have arisen concerning the "Christian" labeling of time, so in some circles A.D. and B.C. have been changed to C.E. ("Common Era") and B.C.E. ("Before the Common Era") respectively.

The question before us is whether we can translate the relative dating of the Bible into absolute dates that allow us to see when these events took place relative to our own time?

For this we turn to other ancient Near Eastern chronological texts. Egypt, Assyria, Babylonia and other neighbors of Israel also kept historical and chronological records. These records, like the biblical ones, are relative, not absolute. However, the key to the transformation from a relative to an absolute chronology comes primarily from an Assyrian text.

The Assyrians kept what are now called *limu* lists. These are lists that record some event that marks a certain year of a king's reign or of some other public official (*limu*). These *limu* lists are found in the Assyrian Eponym Canon that covers 910 to 612 B.C. One year the significant event was an eclipse, allowing astronomers to date this particular year to a specific year in our absolute calendar: 763 B.C. (June 15/16).[2]

To make a long and complex story short, this one firm date allows us to fix a number of other dates in Assyrian history once we start following the trail of all the relative dating done elsewhere. Significant for biblical chronology is the fact that the Bible contains some chronological indicators that cross over to Assyrian history. Further, Assyrian history also mentions some contact with Israelite kings. Perhaps most notable is the reference in the so-called Monolith Inscription to Shalmaneser III's campaign in Syria, where that king encountered an Israelite king named Ahab (853 B.C.), and a reference to the same Assyrian king in context with King Jehu may be found in the Black Obelisk, an archaeological artifact. Once these events are established on an absolute calendar, then other biblical relative dates can be placed in our absolute chronology.

In this way, we are able to establish a date for Solomon's fourth year (see the previous reference to 1 Kings 6:1) to 966 B.C. If we take the 480 years of that verse literally, then the exodus would have occurred in the fifteenth century B.C. (966 + 480 = 1446 B.C.).[3]

The next important bit of information for us as we try to date Abraham is found in Exodus 12:40: The people of Israel had lived in Egypt for 430 years.

Thus we take 1446 and add 430 years and we end up with the date 1876 B.C. for the time that Jacob, Joseph and the rest of the family left Canaan to go to Egypt. If we then add 290 years, representing the time Abraham spent in Canaan as well as the life spans of the other patriarchs, we end up with a birth date for Abraham in 2166 B.C., which then leads to a date of 2091 B.C. for his arrival in Palestine (Gen 12:4-5).

This nice, neat date is not without ambiguity, even on biblical grounds. For one thing, the biblical numbers appear to be rounded-off numbers. But adjusting for this factor would only change the date by nothing more than decades. Second, there are textual variants affecting some of the dates; for instance, the Septuagint understands the 430 years of Exodus 12:40 to cover not only the time in Egypt but the patriarchal period as well.[4] Nevertheless, even with these and other uncertainties taken into account, the Bible itself appears to situate the patriarchs in Palestine sometime between c. 2100-1500 B.C.—the first half of the second millennium.

THE ISSUE

But does the description of the patriarchs fit in with the early second millennium? I ask this question in the light of specific scholarly challenges.

To many scholars the picture of Abraham, Isaac and Jacob seems too far-fetched to be precise history. And even if they were actual people, how could it be proved? They are, after all, not kings ruling empires, nor are they even associated with cities. They would not have left inscriptions, nor is it likely that others would write about them in a way that would be preserved through the millennia. The only witness to their existence is the Bible itself. Not surprisingly, then, confidence in the patriarchs splits into two groups, depending on the level of confidence in the historical veracity of the Bible.

Those who question the actual existence of the patriarchs must come up with an explanation of the texts. The usual response is that the narratives were written during the first millennium B.C. to create an early history about the origins of Israel.

But if this is the case, it is likely that the patriarchs would be described in a way familiar to those who live in the first millennium. We have no indication that first millennium writers could or would try to research what life was actually like in the second millennium. Thus if it could be shown that the patriarchal behavior of Genesis conforms to second millennium customs, especially if these customs differed from first millennium customs, this would provide a strong indirect argument in favor of the Bible's accuracy. This is especially true if it could be shown that the patriarchs are depicted as behaving in ways that would be questionable to a pious first-millennium Israelite. It is in this context that the documents from Nuzi are important.[5]

THE DISCOVERIES AT NUZI

In the 1920s archeologists partially excavated the site of Yorgham Tepe, located in what is today northeastern Iraq. The ancient name of this mound was Nuzi, and among the many important discoveries at this location were some five thousand cuneiform tablets, most written in a form of Akkadian, the language of the Babylonians and Assyrians.

Scholars determined that the Nuzi collection, which included tablets from archives located at the palace as well as the homes of some of the wealthier citizens, came from the midpoint of the second millennium B.C.

At this point in its history Nuzi was a provincial town of the kingdom of Arrapha, a relatively small kingdom with a Hurrian population. The Hurrians are thought to be a people who came from the region of the Caucasus, since their language (as well as the language of Urartu) has similarities with other languages from the region. The Hurrians adopted the cuneiform system of writing, and the texts discovered there have played an important role in the study of the patriarchal period.

These tablets, in particular the ones from private archives, were personal and business texts that reflect the customs of Hurrian society. A prominent Nuzi scholar, Barry L. Eichler, lists some of these customs as: "the contractual stipulations that a barren woman give a slave girl to her husband as wife, the ranking of heirs and the preferential treatment of the designated eldest, the association of the house gods with the disposition of family property, the conditional sale into slavery of freeborn daughters, and the institution of *habiru*-servitude."[6]

These social customs and others are what attracted the attention of biblical scholars to these particular texts. Scholars were immediately attracted to what appeared to be similarities between various social customs from Nuzi and the actions of the patriarchs. Further research promised the possibility of illuminating these customs and perhaps even an empirical way of establishing the date of the patriarchs, either confirming or denying the chronological indicators provided by the Bible itself. In other words, if the customs of the patriarchs conformed to those described in the Nuzi documents, then this would provide an extrabiblical argument that the patriarchs were real people who lived in the time period that the Bible sets them. Of course, the strength of this argument depends on these customs being unique to this time period. If a custom also was current in the first millennium, then it could be that the stories were written in the first millennium and were fictionalized accounts of the supposed precursors to Israel.

Striking similarities. The first generation of scholars who studied these texts was enamored by apparent striking similarities between the customs at Nuzi and the patriarchal narratives. At first glance a number of customs were listed as relevant. These included (1) the adoption of a household slave as heir to a childless couple (see Gen 15), (2) Abraham's marriage to his "sister" Sarah appeared to be reflected in so called "wife-sister contracts" from Nuzi, (3) the possession of the household gods as indicating inheritance rights (see Gen 31:33-34), and (4) the right to sell one's birthright. The scholars who argued these close similarities understood that the Nuzi texts provided evidence for the essential historicity of the patriarchs. They believed the similarities were real and that they were unique to the first to middle part of the second millennium.[7]

To make this viewpoint more concrete, I will describe in more detail one of the customs under discussion, namely, the "wife-sister contracts" that supposedly illumine the relationship between Abraham and Sarah.

Upon their discovery, scholars like Ephraim Speiser argued that the Nuzi tablets explained Sarah's relationship to Abraham as that of a wife-sister.[8] Speiser pointed to one contract where a brother sold his sister to another person as a sister for the price of forty shekels, and to a second (a marriage contract) where the identical original brother sold the same sister as a wife to the same person who had adopted her as his sister, again for forty shekels. So at Nuzi, according to Speiser, this same woman was both sister and wife to the same person. He believed that this clear evidence received support from other less-clear sisterhood contracts. Speiser felt that these sister-wife relationships were a way to bolster the legal ties between the man and the woman.

Speiser used these texts to understand the relationship between Abraham and Sarah. Twice Abraham protects himself from anticipated harm by calling Sarah his sister and not his wife (Gen 12:10-20; 20:1-18). According to Speiser, Sarah's appearance as Abraham's wife-sister is an indication that patriarchal society operated by the same customs as those attested at Nuzi and therefore situates the narrative in the first half of the second millennium. Prominent scholars initially supported this view, and this early optimism is well illustrated by an oft-quoted statement by John Bright, a famous biblical historian of the mid-twentieth century: "[O]ne is forced to the conclusion that the patriarchal narratives authentically reflect social customs at home in the second millennium rather than those of later Israel."[9] Not too long afterward, however, the weakness of this kind of argument was exposed.

Early distortions and actual differences. As time went on and further
texts were studied, it appeared that the initial flush of excitement over
similarities was premature. Once the customs were studied in their individual social context, they proved not to be as close as originally thought.

In terms of the specific custom of the supposed wife-sister institution, it is now very clear that the Nuzi tablets do not help us understand
the relationship between Abraham and Sarah. For one thing, Speiser
had to argue that the later biblical transmitters of the Genesis text did
not understand the ancient custom, and so treated Abraham's ruse as a
deception. But a deception it is. He didn't adopt Sarah as his sister and
as his wife. Further, now that we have eleven relevant Nuzi tablets on
the subject of adoption, we can see that people didn't make sisterhood
contracts with women so they could marry them, but rather they
bought young girls as sisters so they could sell them later as wives (col-
lecting the bride price, which was presumably higher than what they
paid to make them their sister). The original family must have been
hard-pressed for money, and so the buyer bought the rights to sell her
so he could get a larger future compensation, while the seller got an in-
fusion of money right away.

Thus in the case of this particular social custom, further study of the
biblical and Nuzi texts showed that the parallel was not an actual one. In
the case of a number of other customs, further research has demonstrated
that the customs are not unique to the first half of the second millennium,
but they are also found in the first millennium. That this is so prohibits
using the parallels for establishing an early date over a late date for the
production of the patriarchal materials, a point that scholars like Thomas L.
Thompson and John Van Seters, who treat the biblical stories as late fictional retrojections into the past, use to support their point.[10]

Indeed, we need to thank those scholars who pointed out the fallacy of
certain false comparisons between the patriarchal narratives and the Nuzi
texts. But many of them go too far in suggesting that there are no helpful
parallels left. On the contrary, there are still extrabiblical texts, including
those from Nuzi, which corroborate the historical veracity of the Genesis
presentation of the patriarchs.[11] Seeing parallels, whether they are unique

to the first half of the second millennium or not, also helps us understand some of the biblical characters' motivations.

THE BENEFIT OF ANCIENT PARALLELS

Before turning again to evidence that will help us appreciate the historical truth of the patriarchal narratives, we look first at how these ancient texts provide a different type of benefit to our study of the text. That is, they help us understand why the patriarchs do what they do. The following are three quick examples.

Adopting a household servant. In Genesis 15 God comes to reassure Abraham that God will fulfill his promise to provide a child to the couple in their old age. Abraham's initial response indicates that he has lost confidence in God's ability to do this:

> O sovereign LORD, what good are all your blessings when I don't even have a son? Since you've given me no children, Eliezer of Damascus, a servant in my household, will inherit all my wealth. You have given me no descendants of my own, so one of my servants will be my heir. (Gen 15:2-3)

The Nuzi tablets help us understand what is going on here. There we learn that a childless couple can adopt their household servant, who will care for them during their old age and bury them. Afterward, the servant inherits the property. In essence, Abraham utilizes a social custom to try to manufacture an heir.[12]

But God has other plans for Abraham, who will not have to depend on Eliezer to take care of him in his old age. God reaffirms his promise that Sarah and Abraham will have a child of their own. To underline the force of his promise, God undertakes a ritual that again strikes us as strange.

Passing through the divided animals. In answer to Abraham's request that God assure him that he will have an heir, God then instructs the patriarch to bring "a three-year-old heifer, a three-year-old female goat, a three-year-old ram, a turtledove, and a young pigeon" (Gen 15:9). Abraham then kills them and divides all but the birds in half. Then a smoking firepot and a flaming torch pass through the halves, while God reaffirms his covenant promise.

This episode boggles our modern minds. What is going on? The ritual can be illuminated by reference to ancient Near Eastern documents, this time not from Nuzi but from Alalakh, Mari and Hatti. All of these texts are from the second millennium B.C.[13]

The Alalakh text is from the seventeenth century B.C. and has been translated as: "Abban placed himself under oath to Iarimlim and had cut the neck of a sheep (saying): '(Let me so die) if I take back that which I gave thee!' "[14]

The similarity with Genesis 15 is found in the connection between a sacrifice and the establishment of a covenant treaty. In particular, we see the superior party (Abban in the Alalakh text), who is assuring the fulfillment of the agreement, taking a self-curse. God, who takes the form of fire and smoke in Genesis, takes such a self-curse on himself.

However, what is missing here is the passing through the divided parts. For that we appeal to another ancient Near Eastern text, this time from the Hittites. A text that describes a ritual after a military defeat says:

> If the troops have been beaten by the enemy they perform a ritual "behind" the river, as follows: they "cut through" a man, a goat, a puppy, and a little pig; they place half on this side and half on that side, and in front of them they make a gate of . . . wood and stretch a . . . over it, and in front of the gate they light fires on this side and on that, and the troops walk right through, and when they come to the river they sprinkle water over them.[15]

When these and other similar texts are studied together in conjunction with Genesis 15, we can understand the significance of the ritual of slaughtering these animals and God's passing through them. As in the ancient Near Eastern examples, God is performing a self-curse ritual, saying in effect that he will be like those killed and divided animals if he does not keep his promises. He is reassuring Abraham, using a custom known in his day.

Taking a secondary wife. Though God went to extraordinary measures in Genesis 15 to assure Abraham of his intention to fulfill the promise, we see by the very next chapter that Abraham doubts it. He and Sarah are growing older, and he has a hard time believing she can have a child. Thus they avail themselves of yet another ancient social custom to remedy the situation, the taking of a secondary wife, also known as a concubine. Her name is Hagar, and she eventually has a child who is named Ishmael.

Once again Nuzi provides a parallel to a patriarchal custom. In a Nuzi text cited by Hamilton, we read: "If Gilimnimu (the bride) will not bear children, Gilimnimu shall take a woman of N/Lullu land (whence the choicest slaves were obtained) as a wife for Shennima (the bridegroom)."[16]

This reference confirms the fact that Abraham utilized a custom that was current during the first half of the second millennium. By virtue of our knowledge of contemporary customs, we have a clearer idea of what is going through the patriarch's mind. He refuses at this point to trust the Lord, so he tries to manufacture an heir according to the customs of his day.[17]

CONCLUSION

In our third comparative study (see chaps. 4 and 5 for the first studies), we have an issue of a different sort. Here we are looking at the description of the life of the patriarchs against the background of chronologically relevant material. Our aim is to gauge whether or not their depiction resonates as authentic. The assumption is that if the patriarchs were real people, then they will act like their contemporaries. Our conclusion is affirmative. While in the past similarities have been overemphasized, our present state of knowledge encourages the idea that the patriarchs are described in a way that is in keeping with their contemporaries.

PRINCIPLES FOR READING

1. Study Genesis in the light of comparable ancient Near Eastern literature. Information concerning the relevant background information may be found in the best commentaries as well as *The IVP Bible Background Commentary: Old Testament*.

2. Attend to the similarities and differences between the biblical and ancient Near Eastern accounts.

3. Read the creation and flood accounts in the light of ancient parallel texts first before comparing to modern scientific hypotheses.

4. Study the historical content of Genesis in the light of broader ancient Near Eastern material where possible.

FOR FURTHER READING

English Translations of Relevant Texts

Arnold, Bill T., and Bryan E. Beyer. *Readings from the Ancient Near East.* Grand Rapids: Baker, 2002.

Dalley, Stephanie. *Myths from Mesopotamia: Creation, the Flood, Gilgamesh, and Others.* Oxford: Oxford University Press, 1989.

Hallo, William W., and K. Lawson Younger Jr. *The Context of Scripture.* 3 vols. Leiden: Brill, 1997-2002.

Pritchard, James B. *Ancient Near Eastern Texts Relating to the Old Testament with Supplement,* 3rd ed. Princeton, N.J.: Princeton University Press, 1969.

Secondary Literature

Clifford, Richard J. *Creation Accounts in the Ancient Near East and in the Bible.* Washington, D.C.: Catholic Biblical Association, 1994.

Eichler, Barry L. "Nuzi and the Bible: A Retrospective." In H. Behrens et al., eds. *DUMU-È-DUB-BA-A: Studies in Honor of Ake W. Sjöberg.* Philadelphia: Samuel Noah Kramer Fund, 1989.

Heidel, Alexander. *The Babylonian Genesis.* Chicago: University of Chicago Press, 1942.

Lambert, W. G., and A. R. Millard. *Atra-Hasis: The Babylonian Story of the Flood.* Winona Lake, Ind.: Eisenbrauns, 1999.

Levenson, Jon D. *Creation and the Persistence of Evil: The Jewish Drama of Divine Omnipotence.* Princeton, N.J.: Princeton University Press, 1988.

Selman, Martin J. "Comparative Customs and the Patriarchal Age." In A. Millard and D. J. Wiseman, eds. *Essays on the Patriarchal Narratives.* Winona Lake, Ind.: Eisenbrauns, 1980.

Tigay, Jeffrey H. *The Evolution of the Gilgamesh Epic.* Philadelphia: University of Pennsylvania Press, 1982.

Walton, John H., Victor H. Matthews and Mark W. Chavalas. *The IVP Bible Background Commentary: Old Testament.* Downers Grove, Ill.: InterVarsity Press, 2000.

P A R T

READING GENESIS AS GOD'S STORY

■　　　■　　　■

We now begin an interpretive reading of the book of Genesis, always mindful of the principles and background we have explored in the previous chapters. But unlike a full commentary, which has the leisure of lingering over details, I will illustrate a general approach to the text within which more detailed interpretation can take place.

Genesis is the story of God's persistent relationship with his human creatures. He is determined to bless them in spite of their continued sin. This overarching theme of Genesis gives the story its coherence.

I will present the book of Genesis in three parts: the primeval history, the patriarchal narratives, and the Joseph story. These three parts are delineated from each other both by their subject matter and their literary style. In a brief literary space, Genesis 1—11 covers a vast, though unspecified, period of time. The narrative speed slows down when Abraham, the first patriarch, is introduced, and this pace is continued through the stories of Isaac and Jacob as well (chaps. 12-36). The Joseph story (chaps. 37-50) is differentiated from what precedes by the novel-like quality of its narration, in obvious contrast to the rather episodic way that the patriarchal narratives are presented.

It is easy to read these three parts as if they are isolated from each other, but doing so is a mistake. While they each provide their own unique emphases, God's blessing, the loss of the blessing and its recovery is a pervasive theme.

Genesis 1—2, the creation account, describes how God blesses human beings by creating them and placing them in the Garden, where all of their needs are met. Most importantly, they are blessed with a vital and harmonious relationship with God. They live in God's Garden in God's presence.

Genesis 3 narrates the disruption of God's blessing by humanity's willful rebellion. At this point, we see a pattern that continues through Genesis 11 and into the patriarchal narratives and beyond. God consistently judges sin; he does not let human rebellion pass unnoticed. But he does not completely reject humanity either. He pursues them with his blessing. Whether it is through what I call the "tokens of grace" of the stories of Genesis 3—11 or the promises of Genesis 12—50, we will see God's persistent desire to lead his creatures back to a restored relationship with him. In *The Story of Israel,* the authors describe the post-Garden narrative well when they say it is about "how Israel gets back to the Garden, not geographically but spatially," and "how . . . the people of God enjoy the blessing of being in God's presence."[1]

With this overarching understanding of Genesis in mind, we begin our exploration of its three parts.

SEVEN

THE PRIMEVAL HISTORY

Genesis 1—11

Creation in seven days. A man formed from dust and infused with the breath of God; a woman shaped from the man's rib. A snake appearing from nowhere and speaking evil in the Garden of Eden. The sons of God intermarrying with the daughters of men and giving birth to giants. Noah riding out a devastating flood in an ark teeming with representatives of all the animals. A tower that reaches to heaven. People who live almost a millennium. This is just a beginning list of the wonders we encounter in the first eleven chapters of the Bible.

Since they follow a line of descent rather than listing every generation exhaustively, the genealogies of these chapters do not allow us to know when creation took place. Even so, it is certain that the period of time covered by Genesis 1—11 is longer than the time from Genesis 12 (Abraham) until today! No wonder we are left with many questions. Some of the questions are classics: "What about the dinosaurs?" "Who did the children of Adam and Eve marry?" "Who is the snake, where did he come from, and where did he get the attitude?" Some of these questions are unanswerable; the Bible simply is uninterested in them. We can make educated guesses about others. However, in many instances we must allow for some flexibility in interpretation. But unfortunately, the enigmatic passages of Genesis 1—11 have often been the battleground of vicious debates among Christians.

With some trepidation, then, and plenty of humility, I begin with an interpretive reading of the Genesis 1—11 based on the type of research we have discussed up to this point. You will get the most out of your reading of the following section if you also read Genesis 1—11 in a contemporary English translation.

GENESIS 1—2: THE CREATION

The story begins with the account of God's creation of the cosmos and of human beings. The story is told in a way that will underline the tremendous blessing that God confers on Adam and Eve. They aren't just given mere existence but a rich and vital life in the very presence of God.

The Bible begins with two accounts of creation: the first appears in Genesis 1:1—2:4a, and the second follows immediately after in Genesis 2:4b and continues to the end of the chapter. We have already considered the possibility that these two accounts might come from two different sources; however, we concluded that what we have are two accounts from two different perspectives, one cosmic and the other focused on the creation of human beings.

The first account majestically narrates God's creation of the whole of reality. There is an ambiguity, however, in the very first verses. Comparing different English translations (and paying attention to their footnotes) makes the ambiguity obvious. The popular NIV says:

> In the beginning God created the heavens and the earth. Now the earth was formless and empty.

The NRSV represents the other possibility:

> In the beginning when God created the heavens and the earth, the earth was a formless void.

It seems a small difference, but people make a big point of it. The tradition represented by the NRSV implies that a formless earth was present at the beginning of God's creative actions, whereas the NIV suggests what has been called "creation from nothing" (*creatio ex nihilo*).

The truth is that we cannot be certain from the grammar; it could be read either way. Translators take their cues from other considerations. Those who want to understand it like the NRSV does point to the fact that other ancient Near Eastern creation stories (see chap. 4) presume that matter is already present to the creator god. More determinative for those who hold the Bible as the ultimate authority is that later biblical texts (Heb 11:3; Rev 4:11) as well as early interpretations (2 Macc 7:28) understand the creation to be from nothing, not from something that already existed.[1] In any case, even if the text did not definitively speak of the creation of matter from nothing, we would still imagine that the ancient readers would have understood the primordial stuff to be created by God. Where else would it have come from?

Genesis 1 then seems to make a general statement in the first verse, "God created the heavens and the earth," and then proceeds to a more detailed telling of the story in which the first thing he created was matter, which was "formless and empty mass," covered by "deep waters." The Hebrew phrase for "formless and empty mass" is *tohu vabohu*, and I like to describe it as "the blob."

It is from this blob that God will carefully sculpt the world in all its beauty. Indeed, as God exerts his energy in the formation of the heavens and earth, we are to imagine a magnificent artist at work. (Later, after the Fall into sin, the metaphor of the artist is changed to that of a warrior.)

God takes the blob and from it shapes the world as we know it. He does this great work by the power of his word. He speaks, and it is done. The text narrates this as the work of six days.

Many modern readers stumble over the six days of creation. They ask how it could have happened so quickly. It is interesting to note that before the nineteenth century and the work of Charles Darwin the question was just the opposite. For instance, in the sixteenth century John Calvin encountered skepticism concerning the biblical account because it took God so long to create. The biblical account seemed ridiculous to many readers in the sixteenth century because they knew that God could create instantaneously if he so willed.

Of course the difference has to do with the discoveries of modern science. Scientific research concluded that the world is old, the process that brought the cosmos into being took huge amounts of time, and that human beings are relative latecomers to the process and are themselves the product of a long evolution. It seemed that scientific models of creation clashed with the biblical description. But did they really?

Some theologians immediately adopted an apologetic stance and tried to sow doubt concerning the validity of the scientific model. However, cooler heads raised the question of the interpretation of Genesis 1—2. They used the new discoveries as an occasion not to review the truth of the Genesis account but to review whether the traditional interpretation was correct.

Indeed, even a superficial reading of Genesis 1 should lead the interpreter to question whether the Hebrew word *yom* (day) should be understood as a twenty-four hour day. After all, a twenty-four-hour day is defined by the alternation of sun and moon. But these are not even created until the fourth "day"! Attempts to suggest that there were alternative and temporary light sources are really cases of special pleading.

However, the suggestion that "day" does not mean a literal day but rather a period of time also has its problems. This idea is supported by passages outside of the creation account where *yom* appears to be used in reference to a period of time. The only problem with this argument is that these occurrences come in formulas like "day of the Lord." Furthermore, Genesis 1 accompanies the word *yom* with the phrase "and evening passed and morning came."

It appears that Genesis itself is not interested in giving us a clear and unambiguous understanding of the nature of the creation days. This ambiguity fits in with the overall impression we get of the passage, that it is not concerned to tell us the process of creation. Rather it is intent on simply celebrating and asserting the fact that God is Creator.

What is clear is that there is an intentional relationship between the first three days of creation and the last three days. The first three days describe the creation of realms of habitations. The second three narrate the creation of the inhabitants of these realms, so the realms created on day one (light, darkness) are filled on day four (sun, moon, stars), those of day two (sky, water) are filled on day five (birds, fish) and day three (land) is filled on day six (land animals, humans).

Day One	Day Two	Day Three
Light, darkness	sky, water	land

Day Four	Day Five	Day Six
Sun, moon, stars	birds, fish	animals, humans

This sequence demonstrates the care with which God prepares the cosmos for its inhabitants. It particularly highlights the special relationship that God has with his human creatures. The latter extends well beyond the fact that the rest of creation is a kind of backdrop for the creation of Adam and Eve. Consider the following signals from the text that underline the special place of humans in God's creation:

1. Human beings, significantly specified as both male and female (Gen 1:26-27), are created in the image of God. Admittedly, the concept of the image of God is a tricky one to pin down with precision, but there is no question about the fact that it indicates a very special connection with God that the other creatures do not share.

However, all is not lost in terms of understanding the concept image of God either. As Walter Brueggemann has pointed out, the Hebrew word for image (*tselem*) is also used for the construction of royal images.[2] That is, while the king could not be physically present throughout his entire realm, he would set up images of himself throughout the kingdom to remind the people of his authority. In this sense the image of God may be taken to mean that human beings are God's representations in the creation. We reflect the divine glory in the world. Though the exact force of being created in the image of God may escape us, it clearly highlights the special relationship between God and his creatures.

2. The second creation account gives a more detailed description of the creation of the first man, and again the process of his creation shows the

intimate relationship that humankind enjoys with God. Let's first briefly revisit the rival creation accounts. In the *Enuma Elish* (see chap. 4) humans are created from the dust and the blood of a rebellious demon god. In the *Atrahasis* (see chaps. 4 and 5) humans are created to replace the lesser gods who have been digging irrigation ditches. Humans will now do this hard labor. This represents a fairly low view of the status and function of human beings.

On the other hand, the Bible describes the creation of Adam in a way that exalts humans. Indeed, while Adam is related to the rest of creation, specified by the fact that his body is made of the dust of the earth, his special relation with God is highlighted by the fact that his body is animated by the very "breath of life" (Gen 2:7).

When we talk about the creation of Adam being special, we may note that the female is included. After all, the woman is created from a part of the man (his rib or side, Gen 2:21). This indicates that she is his equal; she is not created from his head or his feet. They are joined at the side, so to speak, both created in God's image.

3. After creation, Adam and Eve are commissioned with tasks that clearly show they are God's agents in creation. First, human beings are the only creatures who have an I-Thou relationship with God, able to carry on a conversation with him. They are the ones who are specifically given charge to "be masters" over the other creatures (Gen 1:28-31). A task that is worked out by their tending the Garden of Eden and Adam's naming of the animals (Gen 2:15, 20).

Creation comes to a completion with the introduction of humanity. The first creation account then concludes with the notice that God stopped his creative work on the seventh day and rested. The second creation account underlines the importance of humanity by telling the story again, this time from a human point of view. We do not need to proceed through this account in detail since we have already integrated several important elements from it.

What does the creation account teach us? As we read Genesis 1—2 closely, we note just how little the narrative is interested in telling us about the process of creation. Some interpreters press the text in ways that it does not intend to be read in order to argue against modern scientific conclusions concerning the origins of human beings. It's not that the creation accounts have nothing to say in the light of scientific theories,[3] but that is not its primary meaning. Often in the debate we miss what is truly the concern of the biblical writer. After all, Genesis 1—2 is the very foundation of Scripture, laying down basic and fundamental truths about God, ourselves and the world.

So what is the creation account telling us? God created creation! Genesis 1—2 celebrates God's creation of the universe. The implied consequence of this is that everything is dependent on God for its very existence. Later biblical books insist that those who don't recognize their ultimate dependence on Yahweh are utter fools. This is expressed in a negative way in Psalm 14:1 and Psalm 53:1. It is stated more positively in Proverbs 1:7: "the fear of the LORD is the beginning of true knowledge." Genesis 1 informs human beings in particular of their place in the cosmos. They are totally dependent on God for everything, including life itself.

Not only does the creation account tell us that God created everything, it tells us that he created it "good" (see Gen 1:4, 12, 18, 21, 25, 31; in v. 31, the creation of human beings is called "very good"). This is important because the ancient Israelites, the original readers of this creation account, would not have experienced the world as entirely good. The same is true today. The creation account informs and assures us that the world, as created by God, was good. Evil must have come from another source.

Through this creation account the nature of God is revealed to us in some very fundamental ways. First, God is described from a theistic, not a deistic or pantheistic, perspective. The God of the creation accounts is not a part of creation, he is above it (contra pantheism, which suggests that God permeates all of creation and is not differentiated from it), but God is also present in creation and involved with his human creatures (contra deism, which says God created the world in a way that allows it to operate on its own). In other words, God is both transcendent and immanent.

Furthermore, God is sovereign, self-sufficient and supreme. This radically departs from other ancient Near Eastern religions. These religions are polytheistic, meaning that there are a number of different gods and goddesses, none of whom individually are sovereign, self-sufficient or supreme. They are all rivals, and the world is created as a result of divine conflict (see chap. 4).

In Genesis 1—2 we learn definitively that God is not a sexual or gendered being. In the context of ancient Near Eastern religion, this is a radical conception. After all, the pantheons of Mesopotamia, Canaan and Egypt were composed of goddesses as well as gods. Creation was often envisioned as connected to divine sexual activity. But the God of the Bible may not be legitimately described as male or female. In the first place, Yahweh has no body, so anatomically this is obviously true. Nonetheless, even today many people imagine that God is male on the grounds that the Old Testament uses male pronouns to refer to him.

But Genesis 1:27 announces:

> *So God created human beings in his own image.*
>   *In the image of God he created them;*
>   *male and female he created them.*

This passage does not say that men were created in God's image, then women in man's image. No, both male and female reflect what God is like. No wonder then that female imagery (e.g., mother, Ps 131; Is 66:13; Wisdom (feminine), Prov 1:20-33; 8—9) is used in addition to the more common male imagery for God.

Thus the creation accounts recognize the equality of men and women before God. Besides the significance of the woman's creation from the man's rib, she is also referred to as his helper (Gen 2:18, *'ezer*), a word perhaps best understood as "ally." But whatever the translation, it is important to realize that this term does not imply subordination. Elsewhere this word is often used to describe Yahweh as the helper to Israel (e.g., Deut 33:29; Ps 33:20; 89:18-19 [19-20])!

The creation accounts also establish three fundamental human institutions: marriage, work and sabbath. The fact that they were founded during creation and before the Fall also illumines our understanding of these institutions.

For instance, after Adam was formed and placed in the Garden, he is charged to "watch over it" (Gen 2:15). Paradise was not without labor! We might reasonably surmise, however, that since difficulty was introduced into work because of Adam and Eve's sin (Gen 3:17-19) the original work must have been inherently fulfilling and productive. Ever since the Fall humans have experienced frustration in work. But it's important to remember that that work is not the result of the Fall.

The same may be said for marriage, that intimate bond between a man and a woman (Gen 2:18-25). Marriage involves a man and a woman leaving their parents and forming a new family unit. Their lives are joined together, which is expressed physically through sexual intercourse ("the two are united into one," Gen 2:24). This narrative informs us that marriage, with all its post-Fall problems, is not the result of the curse, but the purpose of God at creation.

Finally, the sabbath was instituted at creation. It is built into the structure of the creation week. God worked six days and then rested on the seventh (Gen 2:1-3). While there is no indication in the Genesis text that humans are supposed to follow the creation pattern, the form of the fourth commandment in Exodus grounds its observation in creation (Ex 20:8-11).

While many issues remain in terms of understanding the nature and present status of work, marriage and sabbath observance,[4] it's important that we take note of their establishment at the time of creation.

Concluding remarks on the creation. Genesis 1—2 in many ways provides the foundation of the Bible. While it doesn't teach us much about the process of creation, it certainly tells us a lot about who God is, what the world was like at the beginning and who we are. In particular, in keeping with the overall theme of Genesis, the creation account tells us that God created humans and blessed them with meaningful and abundant life. Creation is truly a happy story, but as we turn the page to Genesis 3, we see that the joy is short-lived.

GENESIS 3: THE TRAGEDY OF THE FALL

When Genesis was written, the world was already broken by sin. Whether written at the time of Moses or long afterward, people daily experienced harm at the hands of others, and they paid back in kind. The world quite simply is not a nice place. The creation account tells us that though no one can escape the brokenness of world, God did not create it that way. Genesis 3 provides the account of how the world came to be the evil place that it is.

The story begins with the abrupt appearance of the serpent. Questions immediately come to mind, questions that we cannot answer with any assurance. Where did the serpent come from? How did the serpent turn evil? Who is the serpent?

If we ask, What did the original readers of Genesis 3 know about these questions? we would have to honestly admit that they probably didn't have a deep understanding of the serpent. The New Testament identifies the serpent with Satan (Rom 16:20; Rev 12:9), and that does make sense in the light of what we later learn about Satan. But as for how Satan came to be evil, Scripture provides no direct answer. Appeals to Isaiah 14 are not legitimate, for in that case a Canaanite myth is employed in a satire on a Babylonian king. The notion that there was an earlier fall of some angels may be right, but it is based on pure inference and not explicit textual witness.

For our purposes, we realize that it is not important to the story to answer these questions. The serpent represents one who is intent on undermining the authority of Yahweh, and the serpent is not lacking ability, being described as shrewd (a word that is associated with wisdom and is used in a positive sense in the book of Proverbs).

The serpent thus begins to interrogate the woman with questions designed to provoke her. He begins with "Did God really say you must not eat the fruit from any of the trees in the garden?" In response Eve springs to God's defense. Of course, he did not say such a stupid thing. "It's only the fruit from the tree in the middle of the garden that we are not allowed to eat." So far so good, but then she adds: "God said, 'You must not eat it or even touch it; if you do, you will die'" (Gen 3:3).

Really? Or even touch it? Where did God say that? Nowhere! Eve is the first legalist, one who makes up laws that God did not command. There may be a positive intention to legalism: If I don't touch the tree, then I won't eat it. The principle has been applied to many other areas, even today. Among conservative Jewish people it is common never to speak the name of God so that the name is never taken "in vain" (Ex 20:7 KJV). Some Christians say that it is wrong to drink alcohol, though God himself gave it to make people happy (Ps 104:15), in order to keep from getting drunk. Dancing is forbidden in some quarters to ensure that un-married men and women don't get too close physically.

Eve even may have believed her own legalistic interpretation of God's command. Perhaps, then, when she touched the fruit and did not drop dead, she felt comfortable eating it. In any case, the serpent now takes full advantage of her weakness and accuses God of deceiving his human crea-tures for his own selfish purposes. God wants knowledge kept to himself, according to the serpent, "God knows that your eyes will be opened as soon as you eat it, and you will be like God, knowing both good and evil" (Gen 3:5).

What is the "tree of the knowledge of good and evil"? And why would God keep Adam and Eve from knowledge anyway? The best interpreta-tion understands the eating of the tree as the assertion of moral autonomy. In other words, by eating the fruit, the human couple is essentially claim-ing that they know better than God. The Hebrew word for "knowledge" implies experience. By eating the fruit, they now experience evil, separat-ing their moral judgment from God's. Eating the fruit seems a small thing, but it's actually a tremendously wicked act. By doing it, they erect a bar-rier between themselves and God.

But so far in the narrative, we have only described Eve as involved. What about Adam? Did the man get the short end of the stick, suffering a punishment because of the act of his wife? Not at all. He is equally cul-pable, if not more so. Genesis 3:6 makes it clear that he was "with her" during the interchange with the serpent, but he remained silent. He should have interrupted. He should have chased the serpent off. And when it comes down to it, when he is offered the fruit himself, he eats it— no questions asked, no protests given. Adam and Eve together rebelled against their Creator, so they both suffer the horrible consequences.

The effects of the Fall. God had warned them: "If you eat its fruit, you are sure to die" (Gen 2:17). Though Adam and Eve do not immediately drop dead, their ejection from the Garden of Eden means separation from the tree of life. It's now just a matter of time until they return to the dust from which they came.

However, the effects of the Fall go well beyond physical death. The first place the consequences of the Fall can be seen is in relationship, which is so important to human beings. No longer can Adam and Eve stand naked before one another and feel no shame. They cover themselves with fig leaves. Their shame extends beyond a feeling of physical inadequacy and includes a psychological and spiritual estrangement. They no longer experience the same measure of intimate connectedness that they felt before the sin.

But this is not the worst of it. This separation of Adam and Eve derives from a more fundamental disconnection with God. Up to now Adam and Eve have had easy access to and communion with God. But now Adam hears God's voice and runs (Gen 3:10). Their removal from Eden also implies that they no longer can easily be in the presence of God.

But there is still more. God tailors appropriate punishments for all three of the parties. Each of them is responsible for this act, though Adam blames Eve who blames the serpent (Gen 3:11-13). The curses against the serpent, Eve and Adam prick them in the heart of their identity.

The serpent is doomed from this point on to "eat dust," slithering along the earth rather than walking on appendages. But most ominously and weighted with future significance, God pronounces: "I will cause hostility between you and the woman and between your offspring and her offspring. He will strike your head, and you will strike his heel" (Gen 3:15).

In its original setting this passage would have been enigmatic. Who are the offspring of the serpent and the offspring of the woman? How will the serpent's head be crushed, and how would the woman's heel be struck? As biblical history unfolds, we soon see that humankind is split into two groups, the godly and the ungodly. Indeed, we will see this split in the stories that follow in Genesis 4—11 as well as in the genealogies that include Cain and Seth, one notably evil and the other following God (Gen 4:17-26 and

Gen 5). Throughout the Bible conflict erupts between these two groups.

Even though it is unlikely that the original readers of Genesis had a clue about the final outcome of this battle, the New Testament locates its climax in Christ's death on the cross (see Col 2:15). In Jesus' crucifixion, the serpent strikes the foot of the seed of the woman (Christ), but by dying and being raised again to life, he crushes the serpent's head (see pp. 166-69). For this reason this passage has been called the *protoevangelium* in the history of interpretation. In plain English, this is the first announcement of future salvation.

Notice that this curse goes to the heart of the serpent's passions. From the story alone, we can surmise that the serpent is intent on undermining the authority of God among the people whom God created. Why the serpent wants to do this is beyond the information provided in Genesis 3, but the curse reveals that the serpent's goals will not be achieved. Rather the offspring of the woman will eventually destroy him.

God then turns his attention to the woman. The woman is the womb bearer and thus is constitutionally bent toward relationship. It is precisely here that God chooses to punish her. Life will still come from her womb, but at a cost. She will endure great pain in the process. But she will suffer more than physical pain. In an often misunderstood statement, God proclaims that "your desire will be for your husband, and he will rule over you" (Gen 3:16 NIV). The key to understanding the proper force of this part of the curse has to do with the nature of the woman's desire. Too often that desire is thought to be romantic. The woman wants intimacy with the husband, but he responds with domination. The Hebrew word translated as desire here (*teshuqah*) is only used two other places (Gen 4:7; Song 7:10). The first of these is most telling because it is in the same context. In Genesis 4:7 the subject is sin's desire to dominate Cain. In the same way, the woman's desire should be seen as a desire to dominate Adam. Thus this curse describes the power struggle that will dominate the relationship between the genders even to this day.

If relationship is at the heart of the punishment directed toward the woman, work receives attention in Adam's curse. Appropriately for the context of the setting, where Adam has earlier been charged with maintaining the Garden (Gen 2:15), the punishment takes an agrarian shape. As the NLT translates so vividly, "the ground is cursed because of you. All your life you will struggle to scratch a living from it. It will grow thorns and thistles for you, though you will eat of its grains. By the sweat of your brow will you have food to eat" (Gen 3:17-19).

That the woman is cursed in relationships and the man in work certainly doesn't mean that women shouldn't work or men don't care about relationships, but it may indicate where the genders have tended to place their respective deepest significance. However, men also feel frustration in relationships and women too struggle in their work.

The climax of the chapter, however, comes in the final few verses (Gen 3:22-24) where God banishes them from Eden forever. Never again will their life be the same. The blessing of God on human beings has been severely disrupted.

THE PATTERN: SIN, JUDGMENT SPEECH, TOKEN OF GRACE, JUDGMENT

Scholars have noted that the account of the Fall demonstrates a pattern that will be repeated in the four stories that follow in Genesis 4—11 (Cain and Abel, the sons of God and the daughters of men, the flood, the tower of Babel). The pattern narrates (1) a sin, followed by (2) a judgment speech of God. However, before (4) God executes the judgment, he (3) gives them a token of his grace. In these stories we not only see how human sin has disrupted the blessing of God on his human creatures, but also God's pursuit of them in order to restore relationship with them.

We can see how this operates in Genesis 3, the account of the Fall.

1. Adam and Eve sin by eating the forbidden fruit. The serpent sins by seducing them into this evil act.

2. God then pronounces his judgment in the series of curses that he speaks against the serpent, the woman and the man.

3. The token of grace is the clothes that God fashions for Adam and Eve out of animal skins. God encourages them in the area where they express most vulnerability.

4. He then executes his judgment by ejecting them from the Garden of Eden.

That this fourfold pattern may be illustrated by a brief summary of the plot of each of the following stories.

Cain and Abel. After ejection from the Garden, Adam and Eve had children. Two are named at the beginning of Genesis 4: Cain and Abel. These two children are as different as night and day. Cain is a farmer and Abel a shepherd. Though one school of interpretation argues that the story is about shepherds who are putting down farmers, this is unlikely.[5] It is rather a story that speaks of proper and improper attitudes toward God.

At the time of sacrifice, both men bring products of their profession. Cain brings vegetables, and Abel brings lambs from his flock. God accepts only Abel's offering without explicit explanation, leaving later readers guessing. Is it because Abel's sacrifice is bloody? Is it an arbitrary decision?

The answer to this question is subtly presented in the text. The clues are the adjectives used to describe the respective sacrifices. Cain's sacrifice of farm produce has no qualifiers. He brought plain old vegetables. Abel on the other hand brought to the Lord "the best of firstborn lambs from his flock" (Gen 4:4). Nothing is too good for the Lord. This external gift reflects the gratitude of his heart.

Cain's apparent lack of gratitude moves to something darker. So God admonishes him not to be angry. God's rejection of his sacrifice should have led him to change his behavior in positive directions, but his actions get much worse. The sin that was waiting to overtake him ravages his heart. Cain kills his brother, who had received God's favor. The first recorded sin after Eden is fratricide.

Like all who do evil deeds, Cain tries to cover up his crime, but to no avail. God catches him and delivers a judgment speech: "Now you are cursed and banished from the ground, which has swallowed your brother's blood. No longer will the ground yield good crops for you, no matter how hard you work! From now on you will be homeless wanderer on the earth" (Gen 4:11-12). In other words, the curse against Adam has just gotten worse with the sin of Cain.

But in spite of Cain's despicable act, God still extends a token that signifies his continued involvement with him and the sinful human race. In response to his fear that he will be destroyed by others, God marks him with a promise: "I will give a sevenfold punishment to anyone who kills you." While some think that this mark is similar to tattoos that criminals were known to receive in the ancient Near East, because it was a sign of grace this is unlikely. However, the text does not help us understand precisely what form this mark took.

However, what is clear is that humans continue to sin. Yet God continues to judge sin, and also extend his grace by remaining involved.

The "sons of God": Prelude to the flood. The second story that we will examine in the post-Fall period is a true enigma. It is a brief account, but it has captured the imaginations of readers. The nature of the sin is obvious. There is some sort of sexual transgression here. Intimate relationships are formed that are not proper. The first question is, Who are the "sons of God" and the "daughters of men" whose union so angers God?

One popular interpretation understands the union to be between the godly line (represented by the Sethite genealogy in Gen 5) and the ungodly (represented by the Cainite genealogy at the end of Gen 4). This explanation is possible, but it doesn't explain the extraordinary offspring that their relationship produces.

"Sons of God" is a phrase that typically refers to angels (Ps 29:1). If this is taken as the interpretive key to the passage, then the illegitimate union is between angels and humans. This is a better explanation of the children who are called the Nephilim, rightly understood as giants who are "the heroes and famous warriors of ancient times" (Gen 6:4).

The New Living Translation pushes the interpretation in this direction with its translation: "When the human population began to grow rapidly on the earth, the sons of God saw the beautiful women of the human race and took any they wanted as their wives."[6] Intertestamental Jewish literature understood this passage in this way, and it's likely that this event is in the mind of the author of Jude when he says, "And I remind you of the angels who did not stay within the limits of authority God gave them but left the place where they belonged" (Jude 6). In response to those who say that Jesus taught that the angels were asexual, it may be said that a closer look at the passage only says that they do not marry (Lk 20:27-40).

In any case, this story is yet another illustration of the sin of the human race that eventually leads to the flood. It precipitates the judgment speech that will find its execution in the flood itself: "I will wipe this human race I have created from the face of the earth. Yes, and I will destroy every living thing—all the people, the large animals, the small animals that scurry along the ground, and even the birds of the sky. I am sorry I ever made them."

The flood. While the flood is a separate episode in Genesis, the "sons of God" episode is the prelude that gives a concrete instance of the sin that leads to this horrible judgment. After we look at the flood, we will then recognize how the pattern we are tracking also works itself out for the "sons of God" account.

The "sons of God" incident is not the only sin that leads to the judgment of the flood. Indeed, the intensity and frequency of sin that moves God to this drastic step is quite remarkable: "The LORD observed the extent of human wickedness on the earth, and he saw that everything they thought and imagined was consistently and totally evil" (Gen 6:5, see also vv. 11-12). God then determines to destroy humanity, but he does not do so easily. "It broke his heart" (Gen 6:6).

Having noted the sin, the passage then goes on to cite God's speech of judgment: "I will wipe this human race I have created from the face of the earth. Yes, and I will destroy every living thing—all the people, the large animals, the small animals that scurry along the ground, and even the birds of the sky. I am sorry I ever made them" (Gen 6:7, see also vv. 13-21).

The flood, in essence, represents an undoing of creation. Back in Genesis 1, the creation was narrated as God's shaping the formless mass (*tohu vabohu*) by moving back the waters that completely surrounded the world. The flood is thus a reversal of creation.

Whether in our efforts to reconcile science and the Bible we conclude that the flood was universal or local, when we enter the world of the text, we have to conclude that the author felt that everything was covered by the waters of judgment, with one exception: the ark. The problem was universal human sin. The waters themselves covered even the tallest mountains of the region. To picture the scene as described by the author, we must imagine a universal destruction.

But before the judgment is actually executed, God extends a token of his grace to humanity. He informs Noah, a "righteous man" (Gen 6:9), of his plan and instructs him how to build a large boat that will carry him, his immediate family and representative animals to safety.

The narration of the destruction follows in Genesis 7. All but those in the ark are destroyed, and the aftermath is depicted in Genesis 8—9. The transition point from destruction to restoration is signaled by the memorable phrase: "but God remembered Noah" (Gen 8:1). The waters recede, and the ark settles on a mountain peak. After a few more days, Noah released birds to determine that the waters had uncovered dry land.

Finally, on divine command, Noah and all those in the ark departed. Significantly, Noah's first action is to build an altar and offer sacrifices. God then responds by promising not to "curse the ground" again (Gen 8:21). As God continues the work of reconstituting the human race through Noah on what is ostensibly a new earth, we hear many echoes of Genesis 1—2. First, God tells them to "be fruitful and multiply. Fill the earth" (Gen 9:1, compare 1:28). Yet there are significant twists to some aspects of the original relationship between God and human beings that take into account the fallen nature of humanity. For instance, now God allows his human creatures to not only eat plants (Gen 2:15-17) but also animals (Gen 9:2-3). While again we find the language of image of God (9:6, compare 1:26-27), here it is in a context that recognizes social chaos in God's world. The importance of this verse is underlined by the memorable way it is stated. The chiastic structure—"the one who sheds the blood of a person, by a person his blood will be shed"—has a special ring when read in the original Hebrew: *shofekh dam ha'adam ba'adam damo yishafekh.*

This reaffirmation of the relationship between God and humanity is given the name "covenant," first mentioned in Genesis 6:18 and then spelled out in Genesis 9. A biblical covenant is similar to a treaty. God is a great king who enters into a treaty with his servant people, and Noah serves as the main human representative. This is a covenant of creation in which God affirms his intention to preserve the conditions that allow humans to live on earth. On the negative side, he promises to never again bring a flood to destroy human beings (Gen 9:11), and on the positive side he agrees to continue the life cycles of the seasons (Gen 8:22).

Appropriately, the rainbow is declared the sign of the covenant. The sign is a symbol that represents the covenant, and when it appears, it reminds the respective parties of the need to be obedient to its provisions. The rainbow is apt because it is something that appears after the storm. Furthermore, the rainbow may contain an implicit curse that God takes on himself. The Hebrew word for rainbow used here is the same as the word for bow, a weapon. Taken in this sense, God hangs his bow up and its upward direction, pointing at God, may signify that God is saying that he will keep the covenant on pain of death. Of course, God can't die, and that is precisely the point. He can't break the covenant either.

In any case the sad truth is that it's a good thing God promised not to destroy humankind even if they sinned, for it's not long before we hear of additional shortcomings. Bypassing the intriguing story of Noah's sons, we encounter another world crisis: the tower of Babel.

GENESIS 11:1-9: THE TOWER OF BABEL

The story of the tower of Babel proper is found in 11:1-9, but to complete the pattern that described in Genesis 1—11, it is necessary to appeal to Genesis 10 as well. Nonetheless, Genesis 11:1-9 on its own is a powerful illustration of the pervasive and profound literary artistry of the book of Genesis.

The following description is a summary of the excellent literary analysis provided by the Dutch biblical scholar J. P. Fokkelman.[7] Fokkelman's reading of the tower of Babel story has revealed its intricate design. He begins his study by noting word plays throughout this short episode. Certain word groups are bound together by their similar sound: "let us make bricks" (*nilbenah lebenim*), "bake them thoroughly" (*nisrefah lisrefah*), "tar" and " mortar" (*hemar* and *homer*). There is also an alliteration between "brick" (*lebenah*) and "for stone" (*le'aben*). These similar sounds give the story a rhythmic quality that draws the reader's attention not only to the content of the words but to the words themselves. Other repeated words also sound alike: "The place" (*sham*) is what the rebels use as a base for storming "heaven" (*shamayim*) in order to get a "name" (*shem*) for themselves. God, however, reverses the situation because it is "from there" (*misham;* v. 8) that he disperses the rebels and foils their plans. The ironic reversal of the rebels' evil intentions is highlighted in more than one way by the artistic choice of words. Fokkelman lists the numerous words and phrases that appear in the story with the consonant cluster *lbn*, all referring to the human rebellion against God. When God comes in judgment, he confuses (*nbl*) their language. The reversal of the consonants shows the reversal that God's judgment effected in the plans of the rebels. This reversal is also reflected in Fokkelman's analysis of the chiastic structure of the story:

A 11:1 (unity of language)
   B 11:2 (unity of place)
      C 11:3a (intensive communication)
         D 11:3b (plans and inventions)
           E 11:4a (building)
              F 11:4b (city and tower)
                 X 11:5a (God's intervention)
              F' 11:5b (city and tower)
           E' 11:5c (building)
         D' 11:6 (counter plans and inventions)
      C' 11:7 (communication disrupted)
   B' 11:8 (disruption of place)
A' 11:9 (disruption of language)

Unity of language (A) and place (B) and intensive communication (C) induce the men to make plans and inventions (D), especially to building (E) a city and a tower (F). God's intervention is the turning point (X). He watches the buildings (F') people make (E') and launches a counter plan (D') because of which communication becomes impossible (C') and the unity of place (B') and language (A') is broken. Fokkelman's analysis of Genesis 11:1-9 shows on a small scale what is true on a large scale: Genesis is an artfully constructed piece of literature.

After this literary analysis, we can now see the story from the perspective of the pattern of sin, judgment speech, token of grace, and then the execution of judgment. The sin, of course, is the building of the tower. The exact form of this tower is a matter of debate. Typically, and perhaps rightly, the idea behind it is the great Mesopotamian ziggurat, a stepped pyramid that represented a ladder or bridge from earth to heaven. Babylon (Shinar) is explicitly mentioned as the location of this assault on heaven, so perhaps this connection is justified. In any case, whatever the exact form of this building activity, it is an act of pride, an attack on God. It appears to be an attempt to scale heaven and represent human greatness, and it is also a countermeasure to God's desire, in response to the Fall, to scatter the people all over the land.

God will not have it, however, and in a judgment speech addressed apparently to the divine council (see also Gen 1:27), he determines to scatter them by scattering their language. Up to now the passage implies, humans spoke a single language. God would now foil their attempts to scale heaven by dividing their language.

So far the pattern holds steady. However, what about the token of grace? At this point Genesis 10 enters our consideration. In a word God shows grace to human beings by splitting them into language groups, rather than having everyone speak their own unique dialect or completely silencing their voices. In other words, communication becomes much more difficult, but not impossible. Humans can no longer communicate with all other human beings, but there are some who speak the same language, and translation remains a possibility to speak to those outside of our own language group.

Genesis 10 reflects this reality. Unlike a typical genealogy, it really is a kind of ancient linguistic map. The groupings would not stand up to the critique of a modern linguist, but Genesis 10 groups languages that sound a lot alike to the ancient ear. Still, the point stands that communication is possible, even though severely impaired.

The episode concludes by the execution of the judgment. God confuses their language, and the result is that they disperse across the face of the earth, in human clusters to be sure, but no longer able to draw on the resources of the whole.

Persistent sin, consistent judgment, intensive grace. The four stories of Genesis 3—11 thus reflect a similar pattern: sin, judgment speech, token of grace and the execution of judgment. What does this pattern communicate to the reader? First, it shows that human beings are addicted to sin. Human rebellion does not improve or get better with time—it arguably gets worse. And as it gets worse, God is there to consistently judge it. God does not let sin slide. Readers should observe this and be warned. But they should also be encouraged. After all, God does not abandon human beings; he stays involved with them. He pursues them with his grace.

GENEALOGIES

Genealogies link a number of stories. While they may not be the most fascinating parts of Genesis 1—11, they serve many important functions in the narrative, and once we scratch beneath the surface, close study reveals many fascinating insights.

First, we must consider genealogy as a literary form. A genealogy is a list that shows the passage of generations. As such, it signals to us that the writers of Genesis 1—11 want us to recognize their writing as being history. Just because they want us to think it is history obviously doesn't assure a skeptical reader that it gives us a true accounting of the past, but we shouldn't deceive ourselves into thinking that this material was written as myth, legend parable or the like.

Genealogies may be linear, that is, listing one representative per generation (so Gen 4:17—5:32), or segmented, that is, offering multiple descendants per generation (so Gen 10).[8] We must also realize that genealogies are not intended to be exhaustive.[9] Ancient genealogies are not like modern ones used to join an exclusive society or club, say, the Welcome Society, where members are direct descendants of the people who came over on William Penn's ship, the Welcome. In applying to such an organization, it is absolutely necessary to supply a genealogy that does not skip generations. While some biblical genealogies may be like this, many simply desire to show a line of descent, thus skipping generations is not an issue. The consequence of this fact about genealogies is that we must not use them to figure out how much time passed from the beginning of the genealogy to the end. This is particularly important for the genealogy in Genesis 5 since it has wrongly been used to try to determine how much time has passed from Adam to Noah and then to date the time Adam and Eve were created. This "young earth" view is then thrown in the face of the scientific community that believes the age of the earth is immensely old. In truth, the Bible does not speak to the issue of when the world was created.

In addition, as we will see with Genesis 10, sometimes the genealogies are not even primarily concerned with biological descent. In place of descent, the genealogies are rather showing different sorts of important relationships between the members of its list. We learn these facts about the genre of genealogy from a comparison with other genealogies from the broader ancient Near East.

Genesis 4:17—5:32: The genealogies of Cain and Seth. Seth's genealogy immediately follows Cain's, with the express intention that we compare and contrast them. Clearly, we are to understand the first as a genealogy of those, like Cain, who resist God, while the second is a genealogy of those who are on God's side. Augustine suggested that here we see the beginning of a great divide in humanity, anticipated by the language in Genesis 3:15, between a city of man and a city of God.

The Cainite genealogy begins with Cain and concludes with Lamech. The latter is a bigger villain than the fratricide Cain. Lamech kills young boys in return for simply hitting him. The punishment he doles out is thus far worse than the harm against him. Furthermore the specification that Lamech's victim is a young person shows that he takes advantage of those who are much weaker than he is. Lamech also expresses great pride in his presumption that God will protect him like he did Cain. Indeed, God's protection will far exceed (seventy-seven times) what was offered to Cain.

While some of the generations of the Cainite genealogy pass without comment, it is interesting to note that those about whom there is some description are associated with civilization. The Hebrew text as we have it and as modern translations render it associates the first city with Cain, who names it after his son, Enoch. Perhaps though we might speculate that something has happened in the history of the transmission of the text that has removed information without trace. The Sumerian King List tells us that the first city ever built was Eridu, matching not Enoch's name but his son Irad! This is speculation, and we shouldn't change our translations, but textual evidence may one day confirm the fact that Enoch was the first city builder and it was Irad after whom the city was named.

More important, however, is that the Cainite genealogy implicitly encourages us to make the observation that cities are dangerous places. It is a settlement of large group of sinful human beings. This does not minimize sin but rather intensifies it. Other aspects of civilization, music making, metallurgy and herding, are also related to the "dark side" of genealogy, pointing out their potential to be dangerous influences on the human race. Music can seduce, metal workers produce weapons and a primarily agrarian culture is suspicious of those who make their living by herding cattle.

On the other hand, we have the line of Seth, who replaces Abel, the son whose sacrifice was accepted by the Lord. The first thing that we notice about the Sethite genealogy is the incredible life spans that are attributed to its members. The greatest age mentioned is that of old Methuselah (969 years, thus leading to the modern saying "as old as Methuselah"). We wrack our brains trying to rationalize the long lives of these ancient worthies, but it appears that the text wants us to understand them literally. They lived a long, long time—because they lived before sin caused God to radically shorten the human life span. (The Sumerian King List, which mentions the first city, also gives dates to the first kings, and they are exceedingly long—up to tens of thousands of years!)

Finally, while the Cainite line had its Lamech, the Sethite genealogy presents a narrative associated with one of its members, namely Enoch. Enoch is described as someone who "walked with God," which indicates an intimate relationship with the divine. Enoch doesn't suffer death but rather is taken by God. This phrase is mysterious, especially because it appears so early in the history of redemption. Does this mean that Enoch lived forever? Perhaps, though it is unclear. The ancient Near East has stories (Utnapishtim) where the gods take individuals and bestow eternal life on them (Adapa). In any case, Enoch's story underlines the godliness of one strand of humanity in contrast to the ungodliness of the other, represented by Lamech.

Genesis 10. Our treatment of Genesis 10 can be short because we've already seen it in connection to the tower of Babel story. In brief, however, it is a genealogy of a different sort and with a different purpose than those we just studied. Structurally, Genesis 10 is a segmented genealogy; that is, it's not linear. More than one child per generation is given, but then one is typically chosen for expansion into the next generation. This type of genealogy is appropriate for the purpose of Genesis 10, to provide a kind of "linguistic and ethnic" map of the world. It is a phenomenological map based on observed similarities between peoples and languages, not necessarily one that a modern scientific linguist or anthropologist would confirm.

CONCLUSION

In Genesis 1—11 we are introduced to the central theme of the book and indeed one that permeates all of Scripture: God's blessing on his human creatures. It's not mere existence, but an abundant life that is lived in the very presence of God. This blessed condition is characterized by Adam and Eve's life in the Garden. However, human rebellion disrupted humanity's relationship with God. Even so, right from the start (see Gen 3:15), God pursues human beings with his grace. He desires to restore relationship with them and to once again fully bless them.

As we come to the end of chapter 11, we have a significant shift in the narrative. Technically, the new section begins in Genesis 11:27, signaled by the *'elleh toledot* ("this is the account") phrase, the native structuring device of the book of Genesis. This particular *toledot* is that of Terah, which, as we have already observed (chap. 3), means that it concerns Terah's son, the all-important Abraham, father of the faith. We turn now to the story of Abraham and his two immediate descendants, Isaac and Jacob. Here we will see a bold new step in God's plan to bring human beings restored relationship with himself.

EIGHT

THE PATRIARCHAL NARRATIVES

Genesis 12—36

Genesis 1—11 provides the account of the world from creation up to Abraham. These eleven chapters focus on the whole world during an incredibly long period of time. The story begins with humans dwelling in the presence of God and experiencing his blessing. It continues with the tragic story of the disruption of that blessing. But hope persists in God's relentless pursuit of renewed relationship with his human creatures.

With the beginning of the patriarchal narratives (starting at Gen 11:27 with the introduction of the *toledot* of Terah), the narrative focus narrows to one individual, and narrative time slows down as well. God here initiates a new approach to reaching humanity and restoring his blessing on them. He chooses one man through whom he will reach the world.

In essence Genesis 1—11 is the preamble to Genesis 12 and following. The creation account tells us how God blesses humanity with a rich life, while Genesis 3—11 informs us of the willful human disruption of the divine intention. It also instills hope in the reader as it describes God's purposeful pursuit to restore relationship. Indeed, as Gordon J. Wenham puts it so well, "the promises to Abraham renew the vision for humanity set out in Genesis 1 and 2."[1]

Three men—Abraham, Isaac and Jacob—are the patriarchs of Israel whom God uses to establish a people dedicated to his service. Jacob's sons, including Joseph, are not considered patriarchs, as seen in the later reference to God as "the God of Abraham, Isaac and Jacob." This distinction does not minimize importance of the sons of Jacob, who are the "fathers" of the twelve tribes of Israel. It helps explain why I differentiate the patriarchal narratives from the Joseph story.

THE ABRAHAM NARRATIVE

As the one whom God chose, Abraham is the most important of the three patriarchs in terms of development and later theological use.[2] Abraham is *the* father of the faith, the one with whom God chose to enter into covenant. The covenant begins with a demand: "Leave your native country, your relatives, and your father's family, and go to the land that I will show you" (Gen 12:1). This is almost like a second creation account. In Genesis 1 he called the cosmos and also humanity into existence by the power of his command. Now that the divine-human relationship had been broken, he speaks again to Abraham in order to create a new people on whom he will place his blessing.

To understand the force of this demand, we must know something about Ur as well as the land to which God directs Abraham. Biblical chronology situates Abraham in the first part of the second millennium (see chap. 6). We can't precisely date Abraham in relationship to the history of that city, which became turbulent during this time period. However, we do know that Ur was an extremely sophisticated city (its remains are found in Iraq). By Abraham's time, Ur was already an ancient city, founded by Sumerians many centuries before. It was the apex of civilization. To hear the name Ur in the ancient Near East would have the same effect as hearing New York City, London, Tokyo or some other major center of civilization. True, during this time Ur was destroyed by barbarians and thereby lost its prestige, but we are likely to think of Ur at its height. In other words, Ur is a city difficult to leave.

On the other hand, God speaks of "the land that I will show you." Though initially unspecified, it soon becomes clear that that land is

Canaan, now known as Israel or Palestine. Compared to Ur, Canaan was a rough area. Certainly there were important cities at the time—Jericho, Gezer, Shechem and others, which are known from archaeology as well as extrabiblical texts, but they were nothing compared to Ur and the other cities of southern Mesopotamia. Thus Abraham's decision to leave cosmopolitan Ur involved a great deal of trust. But Abraham received promises, and they were formidable:

> *I will make you into a great nation. I will bless you and make you famous, and you will be a blessing to others. I will bless those who bless you and curse those who treat you with contempt. All the families of the earth will be blessed through you. (Gen 12:2-3)*

It is impossible to overestimate the importance of these words for biblical theology. In the first place, they look back to Genesis 1—2, where God had blessed Adam and Eve by placing them in the Garden and telling them to be fruitful and multiply as they subdued the Garden. Through their sin, they were expelled from the Garden. Now Abraham is told he will have numerous descendants, and they will again have dominion over land as well as be both the recipient and the conduit of divine blessing.

These promises also look ahead. They inspire the whole plot, not only of the Abraham narrative and the book of Genesis but of the Pentateuch, the rest of the Old Testament and, indeed, the whole Bible. Here God promises that Abraham will be a great nation and that he will be blessed and a blessing to others.

The promise that Abraham will be a great nation implies two things. First, land. Nations control territory and have inhabitants. And so the promise that Abraham will be a great nation implies that there will be descendants—lots of them.

The second implication of the promise relates to blessing. Blessing seems a rather amorphous concept at first. We know it is good. After all, the opposite is curse, but what it exactly entails is a bit more difficult to delineate. God's blessing on people involves his positive regard for them, the desire to see that they enjoy the truly good things in life. Concerning Abraham, blessing certainly applies back to the idea of land and descendants. He will have them in abundance, and his children will themselves be happy and fruitful. Regarding Abraham's being a blessing to the nations, God will bring good things to the nations through the mediation of Abraham. How these two implications concretely play out is not made specific in this text, and this creates suspense. It keeps us turning the pages to find out.

Indeed, the compelling question of the rest of the Abraham narrative has to do with Abraham's response to the promises. Specifically, how will Abraham react to obstacles that threaten the fulfillment of the promises? Will Abraham display confidence in God's ability and desire to keep his promises or not? As we turn to the rest of the story, we see that Abraham faces a rocky road, and becomes both an encouragement and warning to all of us who read it.[3]

The journey of faith. In obedience to the divine command and in pursuit of the promise, Abraham leaves Ur and strikes out to the west. To travel west from ancient Iraq requires first traveling north along the Euphrates River in order to bypass a treacherous wilderness area. The whole trip is over one thousand miles, but after traveling northwest for a period of time, Abraham (accompanied by his wife Sarah, his father Terah and Lot, the son of his deceased brother Haran) stopped for a period of time in a city named Haran. We don't know how long they stayed in Haran, but it may have been some years. The signal to move on was the death of Terah, who is described in Joshua 24:2 as someone who worshiped false gods.

Abraham, Sarah and Lot then journey down into the Promised Land. When they arrive, they do not put down deep roots. Indeed, they never do during their lifetime. It is not time for Abraham to come into possession of the land that has been promised to him. Indeed, in a matter of a few verses (Gen 12:6-9) Abraham has moved from Shechem to a place between Bethel and Ai, and then finally to the deep south, the Negev. At each place he sets up an altar. In essence, Abraham is setting up monuments to Yahweh throughout the Promised Land.

Again the time indications are not precise, but we are given the impression that soon after his arrival the Promised Land becomes famine land. That is, the land will not sustain life and Abraham has to go to Egypt in order to survive. This famine is the first threat to the fulfillment of the promises. We should put ourselves in Abraham's position. We have responded to God's command on the basis of his promise. We get to the land and find out it is no good. God appears to be a charlatan, at least to the untrusting, and Abraham apparently has trouble trusting.

We see this when he develops a self-defense strategy as he goes to Egypt. He worries that his life will be forfeit because of the beauty of Sarah. Does he trust God to take care of him and protect him? Not at all. He asks Sarah to lie about his status by saying she is his sister and not his wife. While it is true that she is his half-sister (see Gen 20), it's nonetheless a full lie, and he puts the future matriarch in danger. If she is taken by an Egyptian and becomes pregnant or is lost to Abraham, what would become of the promise that this couple would birth a nation?

In any case, God intervenes. The pharaoh himself is enamored by her beauty and adds her to his harem. In return, the pharaoh enriches Abraham, Sarah's supposed brother, with flocks and herds, servants and camels. But God plagues Egypt, and pharaoh discovers why. He then calls Abraham to account and sends him packing back to the Promised Land. Not a stellar start to a journey of faith.

Through Abraham we discover that such a journey is full of ups and downs. Genesis 13 presents a new problem. *Threat* or *obstacle* is probably too strong a word here since the problem derives from prosperity, but it still presents a situation where Abraham has to show whether he will use his own resources to fulfill the promise or not.

Abraham and Lot had both prospered to such an extent that the land with its water and grazing resources won't sustain both of them. They must parcel up the land among themselves. Abraham is in the position of power. He is Lot's uncle, and he is also the recipient of promises. Lot's blessing, in other words, comes through Abraham. The patriarch could have insisted that he gets first choice of land, but he does not. Rather he gives Lot the choice, an amazing show of confidence that this land, all of it, will one day be in the possession of his descendants.

For his part Lot grabs the best land, or at least what appears to be the prime real estate of the day. He chooses that lush grazing area near the two exciting cities of Sodom and Gomorrah. Only a first reader who has never heard the Bible story before can fail to see the irony in that choice.

Genesis 14 is something of a unique chapter in the Abraham narrative. It doesn't echo with the same themes as the rest of the story, so we will examine it separately a little later. Thus we move to the core of the Abraham narrative in Genesis 15—17.

Genesis 15 opens with a divine visit to Abraham. The patriarch's insecurity is signaled by God's initial speech, which addresses his insecurity: "Do not be afraid, Abram, for I will protect you, and your reward will be great" (Gen 15:1). Abraham is not immediately calmed, however, and responds in a way that is curious, at least to modern audiences. He informs God that he still does not have a son, so Eliezer of Damascus, one of his servants, will inherit his wealth.

The finds at Nuzi (see pp. 91-95) have helped us understand what Abraham is saying. Custom at the time allowed for a childless couple to adopt a servant to take care of them as they grew older and in return that servant would receive the inheritance. It's hard to say whether Abraham has actually moved in this direction or is taunting God for failing to follow through on his promise, but in either case it reveals how his mind is working. He worries that the promised nation will never materialize. After all, to be the father of a nation he first has to have a son, and as Abraham grows older this seems increasingly unlikely. He may be grasping at the promise by manufacturing an heir through the customs of the time.

In any case, God immediately assures Abraham that he will still have a son. God not only does so through words but also by action. What follows is strange event that is explained by appeal to ancient Near Eastern custom. We have seen something similar at Mari (see pp. 95-96). When an agreement was reached between two parties, it was occasionally sealed by a self-cursing oath. Through such an oath the partners would call down a curse, even death, on themselves, should they break the agreement.

According to custom a number of animals were cut in half, and the person or persons who passed through the halves were in effect saying, "May I be killed and cut in half like these animals, if I dare break my promises." Strikingly, it is only God who goes through the parts, calling the self-curse on his own head, so to speak. God passes through the parts in the form of a "smoking firepot and a flaming torch" (Gen 15:17). (This form also seems odd to us, but we must remember that often in the early stages of Israel's history God appeared in the form of smoke and fire.) In effect God is saying that if he breaks this promise, he may be killed like these animals. Of course, it is absurd to say that God could die, but it is equally absurd to say God could break his promise.

Here the word *covenant* is used for the first time (v. 18) in connection with Abraham. Though the term is not explicitly used in Genesis 12:1-3, we should think of that passage as reflecting a covenant relationship between God and Abraham, because what we have here is clearly a reaffirmation of the promises of descendants and land first given to Abraham in Ur.

Thus God reassures Abraham, who moves, presumably, from doubt to faith. But for how long? We get no time indicators in Genesis 16, but in Genesis 17, Abraham is grasping again, trying to fulfill the promises in his own way and with the human resources available to him.

In the culture of the day, concubinage was normal, again explained by ancient Near Eastern customs of the time. If a man's wife was barren, he could take a secondary wife, or concubine, and try to have a child. And it worked! Abraham's Egyptian concubine, Hagar, gave birth to a boy who was named Ishmael, which means "God hears," presumably because he seemed an answer to Abraham's prayers.

Again, we do not know the time lapse, but God makes a return visit and initiates the conversation with one more reaffirmation: "I am El-Shaddai—'God Almighty.' Serve me faithfully and live a blameless life. I will make a covenant with you, by which I will guarantee to give you countless descendants" (Gen 17:1-2). He continues by reaffirming the covenant with the promise of countless descendants. God even changes Abraham's name. Up to this point, even though we have been referring to him by his longer name, his name has been Abram, or "exalted father." Now his name will be Abraham, or "father of many."

Abraham, however, initially remains unconvinced. He doubts he can be a father at the age of one hundred and Sarah at the age of ninety. So he still looks to Ishmael: "May Ishmael live under your special blessing!" But God will have none of it. Sarah, whose name he has changed from Sarai at this time (though the significance of this name change from one form of "princess" to another is not as clear) will herself have a child, even though she is long past the time of childbirth.

In conjunction with this reaffirmation, we have the institution of the sign of the Abrahamic covenant. The association of a sign with a covenant was previously seen when God proclaimed the rainbow the sign of the Noahic covenant. But here the sign is circumcision, and as we reflect on it, we can see just how appropriate circumcision is to the Abrahamic covenant.

First, the emphasis at the moment is on the promise of a descendant. Circumcision involves the removal of the foreskin of the penis, the male reproductive organ. This isn't the first time anyone was circumcised. As a matter of fact, circumcision was the rule in the ancient Near East, and when a culture did not practice circumcision of some sort, it was a matter of note ("those uncircumcised Philistines"). Here God takes a known practice and invests it with new meaning.[4] Circumcision was another self-cursing oath. This time, however, it was the human partner who takes on the curse. It signified that if the human partner did not keep up with his side of the agreement, he would be "cut off" and thrown aside just like that foreskin.

It turns out that Abraham isn't the only one to have doubts about the fulfillment of the promise. In Genesis 18 Sarah too reveals her reservations during a visit by three men, who turn out to be heavenly visitors. When one of them, perhaps the one later identified as the LORD himself, assures Abraham "I will return to you about this time next year, and your wife, Sarah, will have a son" (Gen 18:10), Sarah hears this and laughs, thinking to herself "How could a worn-out woman like me enjoy such pleasure, especially when my master—my husband—is also so old?" (Gen 18:12). But these are not the type of visitors from which even a silent laugh or an unexpressed thought could be kept secret. They confront Abraham with the question: "Is anything too hard for the LORD?" (Gen 18:14).

The rocky journey of faith continues. Genesis 18:16—19:38 concerns the destruction of Sodom and the rescue of Lot and his daughters. Abraham tries to protect any godly people of Sodom from destruction. Perhaps here we see Abraham acting like one through whom blessing is brought to the nations. However, in Genesis 20 we get a reprise of the untrusting Abraham, who deceives a king by lying about the status of his wife, thus bringing trouble on that nation.

To keep focused on the promise that Abraham would father a great nation we fast-forward to Genesis 21. Finally, the promised child is born! He is even named laughter, Isaac, because "God has brought me laughter! All who hear about this will laugh with me. Who would have said to Abraham that Sarah would nurse a baby? Yet I have given Abraham a son in his old age!" (Gen 21:6-7).

Why has God waited so long, we might ask? Abraham is one hundred years old, after all, and Sarah ninety. At these advanced ages it is humanly impossible for a couple to have a baby. And as soon as we put it this way, we have our answer. The birth of a child to a barren woman of advanced years shows them (and us) that this special child is a gift of God. As we read on in Genesis (Rebekah and Rachel) and elsewhere in the Old Testament (Samson's mother and Hannah), we see other instances of barren women giving birth to children important to the history of redemption of God's people.[5] We might consider these births a precursor to the most miraculous of all births, when the virgin Mary gave birth to the Savior of all, Jesus.

The ultimate test of faith. Returning to the Abraham narrative, it appears that the plot has reached its appropriate resolution. The promised child has been born! However, such a reaction to the story is soon shown to be premature. God comes with yet a new demand on Abraham's life, one that could hardly have been anticipated. God commands Abraham to take Isaac to Mount Moriah and sacrifice him there.

On the surface of it, this command is absurd. The child is the child of promise. To kill Isaac is, seemingly at least, to kill the promise. What is going on here? While Abraham is not told, we, the readers, learn that this command has a purpose and that is to test Abraham's faith (Gen 22:1).

We have read Abraham's story as a journey of faith and followed his ups and downs throughout his life. With the birth of Isaac he had the confirmation of his faith, but now his world is thrown upside down. But that is not how he reacts. We get no description of Abraham's inner life here. We don't know what thoughts, positive or negative, are running through his mind. We only learn about his actions. In response to the divine command to "Take your son, your only son—yes, Isaac, whom you love so much—and go to the land of Moriah. Go and sacrifice him as a burnt offering on one of the mountains, which I will show you" (Gen 22:2), he gets up early, saddles the donkey, chops wood and sets out for the place.

We might spend our time challenging God's ethics here, but that would be energy wrongly placed. Instead, we marvel at the level of confidence Abraham has come to in his relationship with God. He has doubted through much of his life, but now that he has seen the fulfillment of the promise, he understands that God knows what he is doing.

It's not that Abraham doesn't care for Isaac. God's command seems to emphasize just how much Abraham loves his child, with all the emphasis on Isaac being Abraham's only and beloved son. Indeed, we should also remember that Isaac is no infant at this stage; he's a young boy or even a man who can carry the wood for the sacrifice on his shoulders and who could ask questions about what was going on. It's not that Abraham doesn't love Isaac, but even more, he trusts God to come through in some remarkable way. As Hebrews later puts it:

> It was by faith that Abraham offered Isaac as a sacrifice when God was testing him. Abraham, who had received God's promises, was ready to sacrifice his only son, Isaac, even though God had told him, "Isaac is the son through whom your descendants will be counted." Abraham reasoned that if Isaac died, God was able to bring him back to life again. And in a sense, Abraham did receive his son back from the dead. (Heb 11:17-19)

As Abraham lifts the knife over his son Isaac, God stops him. Abraham has passed the test of faith. God knows and we too know that his faith is real. If God didn't stay Abraham's hand, he would have plunged the knife into his son's body. But instead God provides a substitute, a ram whose horns are caught in a bush.

This story speaks to the generations that follow. It encourages God's people through the ages to wait for the fulfillment of divine promises. We think of those after Abraham and Isaac who hoped for the promise of land. We think of our own situation as we have received the promise of Christ's return and a heavenly home. In spite of obstacles and threats to the fulfillment of these promises, God's people are to continue living in faith and obedience.

ISAAC: THE PROMISE CONTINUES

To be honest, when compared with his father, Abraham, and his son Jacob, Isaac's story is rather nondescript. At least that is true once Isaac grows into manhood and Abraham has died. It is interesting to note that while there is a *toledot* of Terah that focuses on Abraham and a *toledot* of Isaac that focuses on Jacob, no *toledot* of Abraham, which would focus on Isaac, exists.[6] The stories associated with the grown Isaac sound eerily familiar. An example comes in Genesis 26, where a famine strikes the land and so Isaac moves to Gerar, which is under the leadership of the Philistine king Abimelech. As he moves into the area, he introduces his wife as his sister, reminiscent of his father's tactics in Genesis 12 and 20!

The most important point to make about the Isaac narrative has to do with the continuance of the promise. He is the child of the promise, and through him the promise passes down the generations. In God's own words, "Isaac is the son through whom your descendants will be counted" (Gen 21:12). This is signaled through the blessing God pours out on Isaac (Gen 25:11). But most importantly we know that Isaac is the recipient and conduit of the covenantal promises because God says he will be with him and will bless him (e.g., Gen 26:24).

So Isaac is known more as the son of Abraham and the father of Jacob than in his own right. We have seen how he played a pivotal role in the story concerning his father's faith, now we turn to the account of Isaac's son, Jacob the deceiver.

JACOB: GOD WORKS THROUGH THE FOOLISH THINGS OF THE WORLD

The *toledot* of Isaac, in which we anticipate a concentration on the story of his descendants, begins in Genesis 25:19, and true to form it starts with the account of the birth of his two sons, Jacob and Esau. The chaos surrounding the birth of Jacob foreshadows the nature of his life story.

Jacob's birth. Similar to Sarah before her, Rebekah is barren. This signals that the promised descendant is a gift from the Lord, though the narrative does not expand on it as in the case of the Abraham narrative. It duly notes that Rebekah's pregnancy is the result of prayer, and then it tells the story of the birth of twins.

Right from the start sibling rivalry characterizes the relationship between the twins; they fight even in their mother's womb. In answer to their mother's inquiry God announces the reason for the struggle: "the sons in your womb will become two nations. From the very beginning, the two nations will be rivals. One nation will be stronger than the other, and your older son will serve your younger son" (Gen 25:23). Sure enough, when they emerge from the womb, Jacob has a firm hold on the heel of firstborn Esau, as if to pull him back. Their names and descriptions, at birth, as often happens in Hebrew narrative, also forewarn of future events. The oldest is Esau, "hairy," whose hair was so thick that he might as well be wearing clothes. It was also a vivid red color. As for Jacob, his name means "to grab the heel," with connotations of "he deceives."

Birthright. The issue quickly becomes birthright. Through which of the two children will the promise flow to future generations? The text tells the story of Esau's disregard for the future. He is a person of the present, but Jacob is always thinking about how to get the best of the future.

Esau was a country boy. He loved the outdoors, particularly hunting. Jacob on the other hand preferred to stay home. As is typical with such personality traits, the rugged outdoorsman was a favorite of his father, while the one who liked to stay near home was close to his mother.

One day Esau returned from the fields to smell the stew that his brother was cooking. He desired the red stew, which the text explains is the reason for his other portentous name—Edom, "Red," though we might also think it had something to do with the color of his hair. In any case, he impulsively sells his birthright for a simple meal of stew, a sign of things to come.

Whatever the significance of Esau's selling his birthright to Jacob, it apparently did not automatically clarify the inheritance issue since Rebekah and Jacob have to deceive Isaac in order for Jacob to actually receive the blessing of the firstborn. In Genesis 27 we come to the moment of truth, when Isaac confers his blessing on the one whom he thinks is his firstborn, Esau.

Rebekah has other ideas, however; she manipulates events so that her favorite, Jacob, gets the blessing. Why does she do this? What is her motivation? We have already seen that Jacob has gravitated toward her and the home, while Esau is an outdoorsman, to his father's happiness. Furthermore, Esau has aggravated his mother by marrying annoying women. Rather than marrying in the clan, Esau has married local women, and they "made life miserable for Isaac and Rebekah" (Gen 26:35). However, we shouldn't forget that Rebekah heard the divine oracle concerning her two sons, the older will serve the younger (Gen 25:23). The text is not explicit, but more than self-interest seems to be operating here.

Whatever the case, an elaborate ruse is devised to make the blind, elderly Isaac think that Jacob is Esau. The father had sent Esau out to hunt wild game and asked him to prepare his favorite dish. Rebekah heard the conversation and told Jacob to get two goats so she could prepare a dish the way Isaac liked it. Then she took the hairy skin of the goats and prepared gloves and a chest piece for Jacob so Isaac might think that Jacob is hairy Esau.

Jacob is not so sure Isaac will be fooled, and we can see why. First, Esau went out to get wild game. Would the meat of two domesticated goats really fool Isaac? And what about the hair pieces? Will they really deceive Isaac? (Esau must have been hairy indeed!)

It's difficult to read between the lines here, though with Hebrew narrative we frequently are required to do so. Is Isaac so senile that he wouldn't notice? Or is Isaac, whom we know was perturbed by Esau's wives as well, just as happy to see Jacob get the blessing, though in his conflict-avoiding way not willing to confront the hot-head son?

Whatever the motivations, the results are the same. Jacob receives the blessing, and there is nothing Isaac or Esau can do about it. Except, that is, to seek revenge. Isaac has no interest in revenge, but Esau does. So Rebekah again arranges matters so Jacob gets sent away to find a wife among his relatives who still live in Paddan-Aram, what is today Syria. As Jacob sets off, his father blesses him with words revealing that indeed Jacob is the one through whom the promise given to Abraham and Isaac will pass:

> May God Almighty bless you and give you many children. And may your descendants multiply and become many nations! May God pass on to you and your descendants the blessings he has promised to Abraham. May you own this land where you are now living as a foreigner, for God gave this land to Abraham. (Gen 28:3-4)

A dream at Bethel. On his way to Paddan-Aram Jacob has a dream that confirms he is the recipient of the promises, and this time the assurance comes from God himself. As he dreams, he sees a stairway that goes from heaven to earth with angels going up and down the stairway. At the top he hears the following words, the divine confirmation of the fact that he is the one through whom the covenant promises will pass to the following generations:

> I am the LORD, the God of your grandfather Abraham, and the God of your father, Isaac. The ground you are lying on belongs to you. I am giving it to you and your descendants. Your descendants will be as numerous as the dust of the earth! They will spread out in all directions—to west and the east, to the north to south. And all the families of the earth will be blessed through you and your descendants. What's more, I am with you, and I will protect you wherever you go. One day I will bring you back to this land. I will not leave you until I have finished giving you everything I have promised you. (Gen 28:13-15)

In the morning Jacob recognizes that this place is sacred; God had appeared there. He accordingly names the place Bethel, "house of God." He further makes a vow that if his trip is successful, then he will make the Lord his God and will establish Bethel as a worship site. Unfortunately, the future history of Bethel as a place of worship was tarnished by Israel's sin of idolatry (see 1 Kings 13).

At Paddan-Aram. Jacob leaves Bethel and makes his way to Paddan-Aram. His first encounter with the family takes place at the well. Socially, for noncity dwellers, the well functioned similarly to the city gate as a place of public meeting and discussion. Initial meetings take place often at wells in Hebrew narrative (Gen 24:10-27; Ex 2:15-17). Rachel, Jacob's future love, is the first person he meets, and she leads him back to Laban, who warmly welcomes him as "my own flesh and blood!" (Gen 29:14).

Jacob goes to work for Laban, who after a while, offers to compensate him for his labors. Famously, Jacob asks for the hand of Rachel in marriage. After seven years the wedding celebration takes place, but this time the deceiver himself is deceived. Laban slips his less desirable older daughter Leah into Jacob's bed that night, explaining in the morning that this was in keeping with local custom. As Robert Alter points out, when read in the light of Jacob's own deception of his blind father Isaac, we see that he is treated in the same way that he treated his father.[7] Laban allows Jacob to marry Rachel right after the bridal week ended, but he required seven more years of work for her hand. So for fourteen years Jacob toils for Laban so he can have his beloved Rachel.

Though Laban could force Jacob to marry Leah, he could not force him to love her. However, since she is "unloved" (Gen 29:31), the Lord allows her to have children, indeed a number of children. Rachel, on the other hand, can't conceive. The sisters' rivalry degenerates into a contest over who could provide their husband with more children. Rachel got into the act through providing Jacob with a concubine, and Leah responded in kind when it appeared that her own womb was slowing down. Finally, Rachel herself has a child, Joseph, who will be the focus of the final chapters of Genesis.

Of course, these children, twelve when it is all over, are weighted with significance concerning the future history of God's people. They, including Joseph in the name of his two sons, Manasseh and Ephraim, will father the twelve tribes of Israel. Soon, as we will note below, Jacob himself will have a name change. At the end of his life, he will be called Israel. Thus Israel fathers the twelve tribes.

Jacob's name change takes place after the fourteen years of service in return for his two wives. As Laban's character is revealed further in the narrative, we see that he exploits those around him, in particular Jacob.

If Jacob's wives agree on anything, it's that it is in their best interest to get out of town, so they encourage Jacob to follow the Lord's prompting to go back to his family in the land of promise.

But before he leaves, Jacob takes steps to enrich himself at the expense of Laban. Apparently Laban has swindled Jacob on more than marriage partners. Jacob has worked hard for his uncle without adequate compensation. On threat of leaving, Laban finally agrees to pay Jacob. After all, because the Lord is with Jacob, Laban has grown rich. As we have seen and will continue to see, God blesses those who are connected to those who are in covenant relationship, perhaps a foretaste of how God will bless the nations through Abraham.

In any case, Jacob devises a means of payment that he thinks will gain him the material prosperity he deserves but that Laban views as yet another opportunity to exploit his nephew. Jacob claims all the nonwhite—whether dark, speckled or spotted—sheep. Laban stealthily removed these sheep from his flock and gave them into the care of his sons at a distance. So Jacob remained in charge of Laban's flock which "miraculously" turned all white overnight.

But Jacob had a plan of his own. He devised sticks or poles that were streaked, alternating white and dark, like the type of sheep he wanted. He put those near the watering area, and as Laban's white sheep came to drink, they mated and "gave birth to young that were streaked, speckled, and spotted" (Gen 30:39). Jacob's share of the flock grew larger and stronger, while Laban's diminished.

How did this happen? What was it about Jacob's method that led to this great result? Nothing. This seems to have been a rural legend that sheep that mated in front of something that was streaked would be streaked themselves. Nothing in modern science would lead us to think that there is anything to Jacob's procedure. That leads us to one conclusion: God caused this to happen, so Jacob could get his fair share (see Gen 31:9).

Obviously, Laban and his sons were none too pleased about this turn of events, and they made their displeasure known to Jacob. In reaction Jacob tells Rachel and Leah that they should prepare to escape from Paddan-Aram. The sisters don't agree on much, but Laban is apparently the type of father who doesn't generate loyalty, at least among his daughters. They readily agree to Jacob's plan.

Return to the Promised Land. Jacob's desire to flee is undergirded by a divine oracle, which commanded him: "Return to the land of your father and grandfather and to your relatives there, and I will be with you" (Gen 31:3). They steal out secretly, but after three days Laban discovers that they are gone and sets out in hot pursuit. God warns Laban the night before he catches up to Jacob, though, not to mistreat Jacob. This threat explains Laban's hesitation to act harshly with Jacob, but he still asks probing questions. Certainly Laban is being untrue when he says that his biggest disappointment was to not be able to throw a going away party for them all. For years he has gouged Jacob and his two daughters. But he does accuse Jacob of something serious, namely, the theft of the household gods.

This episode remains enigmatic to modern readers. Household gods were a remnant of what we expect to be Jacob's pagan past, and we learn that he had nothing to do with the theft. Rachel has stolen these representations of deity and she gets away with it, but why? In his commentary, Hamilton discusses the major options, which include the possibility, based on texts from ancient Nuzi and Emar, that possession would determine inheritance rights. But it may simply be that Rachel was upset with her father and wanted to strike back at him by taking something of high value to him.[8]

In any case, Jacob and Laban reach a resolution, and the passage concludes with a treaty ritual where Jacob and Laban agree to respect the boundary between them. This resolution anticipates an even more fearful conflict that is about to follow, namely, the old rivalry between Jacob and Esau.

The last time we saw Esau, he was simmering in a stew of revenge against Jacob, who had stolen the paternal blessing (Gen 27:41-46). An indication of divine approval of Jacob's return may be behind the one-verse notice of Jacob's encounter with angels at a place he names Mahanaim "two camps," exclaiming "This is God's camp!" (Gen 32:1-2).

Perhaps emboldened by this event, Jacob alerts Esau, who is now living in Edom, named after him and located to the southeast of the Dead

Sea across from Palestine proper. Jacob words his message very carefully and humbly. He gets, however, an unwanted answer in the form of a report of an oncoming army of four hundred men heading his way—Esau's cohort.

Shaken, Jacob takes action, beginning with prayer. He divides his holdings and household into two parts, with the thought that one might escape if the other comes under attack. He then sends ahead of both groups a series of gifts, hoping to pacify Esau's presumed anger.

After setting up this response, Jacob then spends a very uneasy night during which one of the most memorable as well as enigmatic encounters of the entire Bible takes place. While alone, an unnamed "man" engages the patriarch in a wrestling match. This struggle lasts the entire night. It appears a draw. Though the man has knocked Jacob's hip joint out of its socket (which in Gen 32:32 is given as an explanation for why Israelites do not eat the tendon near the hip socket), Jacob appears to have a tight grip on him. The man appeals to Jacob to let him go before dawn arrives. We aren't told the significance of the appearance of dawn, thus increasing our perplexity as well as our curiosity. Who is this "man"?

Jacob refuses to let him go until the man blesses him. Why does Jacob care? We don't know yet, because we still aren't sure who this man is. Jacob, however, must know the significance of his wrestling partner, though the next interchange shows that he doesn't know his name.

In this interchange, the man appears to bless Jacob by a name change. The "one who grasps the heel," the "deceiver" becomes "Israel." Of course, the importance of this name change is immediately apparent. Israel is the name of the nation that will flow from Jacob's seed. What the name means is not perfectly obvious, but the best proposal understands the name to mean "God fights." This interpretation is appropriate both to the situation in Genesis 32 as well as to the future of the nation Israel, for which God often fights and occasionally fights against. It's also appropriate to the immediate context because, though the man doesn't give his name to Jacob, Jacob knows that it is God himself. In other words, the man doesn't give his name, Yahweh, but Jacob knows it is his God, the God of his father Abraham.

Many questions echo in our minds after reading this passage. Why does God fight Jacob? Why do they apparently fight to a standstill? Why doesn't God give his name? Why does God have to leave before morning light? We will have to live with many of these questions unresolved. The text however is significant in characterizing future Israel as a place for whom and against whom God will come as a warrior. It also teaches other readers that God is someone who calls for our active engagement. Someone who honors us in the struggle as long as we don't let go.

For Jacob the divine struggle sets the scene for the human struggle that follows. Esau's apparent army heading from the south finally encounters Jacob's entourage coming from the north. Jacob has divided his family by relational priorities; those in back are closest to Jacob's heart. The first to meet Esau is the group composed of his concubines and their children (Bilhah: Dan, Naphtali; and Zilpah: Gad, Asher). After them came a group that included Leah and her children (Reuben, Simeon, Levi, Judah, Issachar, Zebulun, Dinah), and finally, behind everyone else, Rachel and her prized son, Joseph. As expected, and nonetheless perhaps admirably, Jacob precedes them all and meets Esau at the front. Unexpectedly, and definitely admirably, Esau runs and embraces Jacob.

The most frustrating aspect of this narrative is the lack of explanation concerning motives. Though typical of Hebrew prose, here it makes the narrative particularly opaque to the modern reader. Why has Esau softened toward Jacob? Is it because of the gifts and Jacob's humility? He at first refuses the gift, but this may simply be ancient Near Eastern protocol, which Jacob understands as he forces it on Esau.

But what comes next in the story is even more difficult. Esau tells Jacob to follow him home, by which he means to Edom. Jacob says he needs time and will follow at a slower pace. Esau then offers to leave him guides, which Jacob politely refuses saying it is unnecessary. Esau then leaves, and Jacob never goes to Edom, instead he travels to Shechem and settles down for what he hopes to be a while. The only time we know that Jacob sees Esau again is when they together bury their father Isaac (Gen 35:29). The latter is simply stated as a matter of fact, but no animosity appears to exist between them.

The text allows for any number of possible reconstructions. But that is the problem. Which is most likely? Did Jacob go to Edom for a while, the text not mentioning it? Who knows? It is better not to speculate. Jacob is successfully back in the land. And even though Esau is not a present danger, more threats are soon coming.

In the land. In Genesis 34 we learn of an episode that has both near and distant future ramifications. Most of the focus has been on the sons of Jacob and his wives, but the narrative has mentioned one daughter, Dinah. In text we learn about an event in Dinah's life, but nothing really about her own reactions to the events. The focus is on the actions of two of Jacob's sons, Simeon and Levi.

It appears that Jacob's extended family had good relationships with the native inhabitants. Dinah was in the habit of spending time with the local girls and thus came to the attention of Shechem, the son of the local ruler, Hamor.

Most English translations understand that Shechem violated her by raping her. This indeed may be the case, but the Hebrew is more ambiguous. The relevant verb is better translated "humbled" her, which leaves it a little more open whether or not he forced himself on her. It may be that he seduced her so that he left her in a humbled circumstance, being an unmarried woman who has slept with a man. Whatever the exact nature of the offense, from the Hebrew perspective, it was a matter of defilement, and something that required response (Gen 34:5).

What becomes very clear, however, is that whether he forced himself on her or not, "he fell in love with her, and he tried to win her affections with tender words" (Gen 34:3). Did he succeed? Again, we do not know, since we never hear this story from Dinah's perspective. In any case, Shechem proposed marriage to Dinah through the proper channels of the culture, namely, her father and brothers.

But the text makes abundantly clear that her brothers are upset about the sex and the marriage proposal, and they want revenge. Two brothers in particular, Levi and Simeon, are singled out as particularly aggrieved at what happened to their sister. Their plan was as crafty as it was deceptive and malicious.

Though not stated explicitly, it is highly likely that Jacob's family was vastly outnumbered by the native inhabitants, but Levi and Simeon (Dinah's full brothers, since they all had Leah as their mother) devised a way to more than level the playing field. They acted like they agreed to the marriage on one condition, that the inhabitants of the land undergo circumcision, a painful and debilitating operation.

Shechem and his father, on behalf of all their people, accept this condition. Perhaps their willingness to undergo this procedure indicates just how authentic Shechem's love was for Dinah as well as his acceptance of Jacob's family to integrate with them.

But the demand was a ruse. Levi and Simeon had absolutely no interest in allowing the marriage to go ahead. After the circumcision, when Shechem's men were in an extremely weak condition, Levi and Simeon went through the town and killed them.

Trying to figure out the attitude of the narrative toward this act is not cut and dried. Jacob is angry: "You have ruined me! You've made me stink among all the people of this land—among all the Canaanites and Perizzites. We are so few that they will join forces and crush us. I will be ruined, and my entire household will be wiped out!" (Gen 34:30). Furthermore, Jacob carries a grudge against these two sons to the grave (see pp. 159-60).

However, the narrator allows the two sons to have the last word as they respond to Jacob's tirade: "But why should we let him treat our sister like a prostitute?" (v. 30). In addition, the offer to integrate Jacob's family with the inhabitants of Shechem would have diluted the covenant family in a way that would have undermined the fulfillment of the promise of descendants. Perhaps we are to think of God using an evil act to bring about good, in this case the preservation of the purity of the covenant line.

Jacob and the family, of course, immediately leave the town of Shechem and head down the central ridge route to Bethel, the place where he had the vision of the ladder to heaven. However, before proceeding, Jacob issues a call to his household to get rid of their pagan idols. He is now going to a sacred place, and he also emphasizes what we have seen is the central theme of the covenant, that is that God "has been with me wherever I have gone" (Gen 35:3). And once he reaches Bethel, God renews the covenant promises that he had given to Abraham and now is applying to his son Jacob (Gen 35:11-13).

With Jacob now in the Promised Land, his narrative begins to wind down. But first there will be one more child, this time born to his favorite wife, Rachel. However, this child cost Rachel her life, and as she died she named him Ben-oni "son of my sorrow" (Gen 35:18). But after her death and burial, Jacob renamed this last son Benjamin, "son of my right hand." Now all twelve sons of Jacob, renamed Israel, are born:

- Leah's children: Reuben, Simeon, Levi, Judah, Issachar and Zebulun
- Rachel's children: Joseph and Benjamin
- Bilhah's (Rachel's concubine) children: Dan and Naphtali
- Zilpah's (Leah's concubine) children: Gad and Asher

The *toledot* of Isaac comes to an end with his death after the return of his son Jacob (Gen 35:27-29). We are now prepared for the next in the series of descendants through whom the promise is passed down, namely, the *toledot* of Jacob, which will focus on Joseph.

As a transition, however, we have the *toledot* of Esau (Gen 36). In Genesis 25 there is a short narration about Ishmael, and now we have one concerning Esau, both descendants of patriarchs but from the nonchosen line. By including these short lists of the descendants of Ishmael and Esau (as well as a list of the rulers of the Edomites who descended from Esau), we learn that God cares for these people even though they aren't directly related to his redemptive strategy begun with Abraham.

CONCLUSION

The patriarchal narratives have a different character than the chapters that precede them. Narrative time has slowed and narrative space has narrowed. Rather than quickly surveying the whole world and a long period of time, the focus is now on one man and his descendants. God has been persistently gracious to humanity as a whole even though the humans continue to sin against him. Now he chooses one person through whom he will restore the blessing to the whole world. The story of the patriarchal narratives is the account of how Abraham, Isaac and Jacob respond to the God who through them pursues relationship with all of humanity.

The last part of Genesis turns to the story of the twelve sons of Jacob by telling the story of one of them, Joseph.

NINE

THE JOSEPH STORY

Genesis 37—50

We now come to the final *toledot* of Genesis, the *toledot* (or "family history") of Jacob (Gen 37:2). In keeping with the pattern that we have seen thus far, the *toledot* of Jacob focuses on Jacob's children. Of all the sons of Jacob, it's Joseph whose story we hear most fully, though we will note a short interruption with a story of Judah (Gen 38).

I will call this section the Joseph story after its main protagonist. One of the first things scholars notice as they begin reading the Joseph story is the change in literary type and quality. While the patriarchal narratives consist of loosely connected and short episodes, the Joseph story has the character of a short story or novella. Though there are different scenes, there is more coherence to the plot than we have seen so far. There is also coherence of theme, noted in part by the common use of the term *bless* in the story. Not only is Joseph blessed, but those around him often are as well. After all, God was with him.

Remember, Joseph is not one of the patriarchs. Later generations will speak of the "God of Abraham, Isaac and Jacob." Notice that Joseph isn't included in this list. The Joseph story provides a bridge between the patriarchs and the exodus account, giving explanation as to how the Israelites arrived in Egypt in the first place. Though not a patriarch per se, Joseph is clearly the recipient of the covenantal promises given to Abraham. We will often hear that God was "with him," blessing him and those in his presence.

The theme of the Joseph story (Gen 50:19-20). To truly understand the Joseph story we should begin near the end, for Joseph himself utters the theme of his life. After the death of Jacob, the eleven brothers, who previously had mistreated their now powerful brother Joseph, are worried that Joseph has waited until this moment to take his revenge on them. They offer to serve him provided that he doesn't hurt them. Joseph is offended and responds by saying: "Don't be afraid of me. Am I God, that I can punish you? You intended to harm me, but God intended it all for good. He brought me to this position so I could save the lives of many people. No, don't be afraid. I will continue to take care of you and your children" (Gen 50:19-20). Indeed, as we reflect on the life of Joseph as told in Genesis 37—50, we are struck by the truth of this statement. From a human perspective Joseph's life seems like a series of hard knocks with no meaning. However, Joseph understands that his life has tremendous meaning.

Joseph in Canaan. We see the pattern unfold from the very beginning. In Genesis 37 Joseph is seventeen years old and his father's favorite. He was the son of his father's beloved wife Rachel, while the others were offspring of Leah or one of the concubines. The preferential treatment that Joseph received was symbolized by the gift of a garment. By popular understanding, this coat is "multicolored," while the Hebrew word suggests that it actually was "long-sleeved." In any case, it was special and pointed to Joseph as the favorite. Accordingly, his brothers hated him.

From what we learn about him at this time, Joseph apparently did nothing to help his case with his brothers. For instance, he had two dreams that he interprets to point to his future role over them. Granted, these dreams are legitimately of divine origin, and Joseph honestly reports them. But they come across as a putdown of his older brothers, so that even Jacob is taken back by Joseph's dreams.

In the first dream all of the brothers are tying up bundles of grain. The one Joseph bundles suddenly stands up, and all the others bow before it.

The second dream takes on cosmic dimensions. Here the sun (representing his father), the moon (representing his mother) and eleven stars (representing his brothers) bow before him. For a boy already intensely disliked because of his father's favoritism, these speeches were almost literally the kiss of death.

The next scene begins as the brothers go to shepherd their father's flock near Shechem, while Joseph stays home, likely another indication of favoritism. After a while Jacob sends Joseph to them. When the brothers see him at a distance, they quickly plot to get rid of him. The majority want to throw him into a pit and let him die there. Reuben, the oldest, plans to come back and get him out, but apparently he isn't there later when a group of Ishmaelite traders happen by. Judah, seeing an economic opportunity, convinces his brothers that they would be better off selling Joseph. Thus the Ishmaelites purchase Joseph, and off he goes to Egypt.

Indeed, off to Egypt, where he will be in a position to help the descendants of Abraham in a future crisis. *The brothers meant it for evil, but God meant it for good, for the saving of many.*

Meanwhile, the brothers fabricate the death of Joseph, so it will look to Jacob as if he was eaten by a wild animal. When informed of this, Jacob collapses in grief.

A SHORT INTERLUDE: JUDAH AND TAMAR

Right after the first chapter devoted to Joseph, we have a momentary interruption to his story. After Joseph's sale to Potiphar, an officer of Pharaoh, the scene shifts to a story concerning his brother Judah. This abrupt transition (and after it, the equally abrupt return to Joseph) is odd to modern readers and begs explanation. That a story about Judah is found in the *toledot* of Jacob is not a problem, but why here, and why now? We don't know. Judah, of course, is the father of an important tribe, and Joseph will be the progenitor of two tribes: Ephraim and Manasseh. Perhaps a contrast is being drawn, but for what purpose is not at all clear.

The story does not put Judah in a positive light. In the first place Judah married a Canaanite woman, reminding us of Esau, whose marriage to Hittite and Canaanite women (see particularly Gen 28:7) was so displeasing to his parents. It is perhaps not surprising that three rather wicked sons came from this union. Er, the firstborn, died because of his wickedness, leaving his wife Tamar a widow. According to law, which is later articulated at the time of Moses (see Deut 25:5-10), it was the duty of a deceased man's brother to marry his widow and have a child with her, and the child will take the name of the dead man and ultimately inherit his land and property. This law, sometimes called the levirate, after the Latin word for brother-in-law, is vividly portrayed in the book of Ruth as Boaz takes on these duties in regard to Ruth.

Judah obeyed the law at first, ordering Onan to fulfill this duty. However, for selfish reasons, Onan refused to impregnate her (Gen 38:9). For this reason God took Onan's life. The next in line was Shelah, but now Judah balks. He deceitfully tells Tamar that he will give her to Shelah once he gets old enough, but really Judah has no intention of doing so since he now fears for his son's life. He attributes the death of his sons to Tamar, whom he considers a kind of black widow, where really the blame is to be laid at the feet of his wicked sons.

The story now takes an unexpected turn. Once Tamar determines that Judah has no intention of giving her to Shelah, she takes drastic measures. What did she really have to lose? The fate of a widow without child is not a pleasant one in ancient Israel. She dons the garb of the prostitute, which included a veil that hides her identity. She takes up her position at the road into the town, and, surprise, Judah ends up hiring her for her services. Having "left his wallet at home," Judah promises to send payment to this woman who is nameless to him. He leaves his identification seal, his cord, and walking stick with her as a guarantee. However, when he later tries to pay her, she is not there.

As a result of this liaison, Tamar gets pregnant. When Judah hears of her condition, he wants to throw the book at her. She has disgraced the family and must accordingly die. However, when confronted, she produces the identification (the seal and walking stick) of the man who impregnated her. Judah immediately recognizes that he's the man and that he's at fault for keeping his son from her.

The text then ends with the birth of the sons of that union, the twins who will carry forward the line of Judah. Their names come from the circumstances surrounding their birth. One child sticks his hand out first and the midwife ties a scarlet threat around his wrist, but then he withdraws the hand back into the womb, and the other child is born first. The latter is named Perez "breaking out," since he was first out, and the second was Zerah, "scarlet," since he was born with a scarlet thread around his wrist.

JOSEPH IN EGYPT

Just before the Judah and Tamar story "interrupted" the Joseph narrative, we had learned that the Ishmaelite/Midianite traders sold Joseph to Potiphar, described as the "captain of the palace guard" (Gen 37:36). In Genesis 39 we see how God makes his presence known to Joseph through the prosperity that comes to Potiphar's household. The story opens with a statement to that effect: "The LORD was with Joseph. So he succeeded in everything he did as he served in the home of his Egyptian master. Potiphar noticed this and realized that the LORD was with Joseph, giving him success in everything he did" (Gen 39:2-3). Because of the blessing that came through Joseph's presence in his household, Potiphar gave him increased responsibility and also granted him a large measure of trust.

Joseph thrown in jail. Everything was going well until Potiphar's wife began to show great interest in Joseph. Attentive readers know that something is about to happen when they hear a reticent narrator uncharacteristically give a physical description of a character (see pp. 65-66): Joseph is pictured as "a very handsome and well-built young man" (Gen 39:6).

The next thing we know, Potiphar's wife is trying to lure him into her bed. Joseph reacts in precisely the right way. He refuses her attentions. His motivation is beautifully expressed: "Look, my master trusts me with everything in his entire household. No one here has more authority than I do! He has held back nothing from me except you, because you are his wife. How could I ever do such a wicked thing? It would be a great sin against God" (Gen 39:8-9). In other words, Joseph is the epitome of the wise man as described in Proverbs 5—7!

Reading the Joseph narrative in the light of those verses, we would fully expect Joseph to reap the rewards of wise behavior. The fool who gives in to such seductions suffers. The wise man who avoids the promiscuous woman is blessed with life and riches. But this is not what happens. The spurned woman turns her wrath on Joseph by framing him for rape.

Confronted with her account of events Potiphar takes out his anger on Joseph, sending him to jail. The fact that Joseph is given a jail term rather than killed may be an indication that Potiphar knew something was fishy about his wife's story. However, the important point is that Joseph is sent to the royal prison, which brings him into contact with prisoners who have had contact with the pharaoh, leaving the reader with the impression that maybe something positive will come out of this apparently bad situation.

The cupbearer and the baker. As happened with Potiphar's household, the prison flourished with Joseph's arrival there (Gen 39:23), and Joseph came to know two officials from Pharaoh's court who were imprisoned for an unspecified offense against their master. While having rather domestic sounding titles (cupbearer and baker), it would be wrong to think of these as unimportant officials. These offices are very important and intimately connected to the king. (This is certainly true in the case of the cupbearer, see Neh 1:11.) The cupbearer was a confidante of the king, trusted to the point of being his food tester, guarding the king against poisoning.

In his relationship with the cupbearer and the baker, Joseph's talent as a diviner comes to the fore. Specifically, he is a dream interpreter. We have already witnessed Joseph's propensity to get messages from God via dreams, but now he interprets the dreams of others.

Divination is frowned on elsewhere in Scripture (Deut 18:10), but what is prohibited is the type of divination that does not depend on God for the interpretation. We note this in the contrast between the wise men of Babylon and Daniel as they interpret Nebuchadnezzar's dream of a multimetalled statue in Daniel 2. Joseph makes it clear that "interpreting dreams is God's business" (Gen 40:8); he is simply the conduit of God's wisdom in this case.

The cupbearer goes first. He sees three grape vines that blossom. He squeezes the grapes and gives their juice to Pharaoh. Joseph interprets this to mean that three days from that moment the cupbearer will be restored to his position. The baker takes heart from this positive message and relates his own dream. He too had a dream involving the number three, in his case three baskets of pastries that were on his head. The top basket was for Pharaoh, but the birds came and ate the pastries. Joseph then gives the bad news to the baker. In his case the message is that the king will cut off his head and impale his body on a pole. The birds will come and eat his corpse.

Everything turned out just as Joseph had interpreted. Three days later was pharaoh's birthday. He released his two servants from jail. The cupbearer was restored to his previous position, but the baker was beheaded.

When he interpreted the cupbearer's dream, Joseph urged him: "Please remember me and do me a favor when things go well for you. Mention me to Pharaoh, so he might let me out of this place" (Gen 40:14-15). But again Joseph is the recipient of ill treatment when the cupbearer promptly "forgot all about Joseph, never giving him another thought" (Gen 40:23). It appears that people intend evil or, in this case, just ignore Joseph with the same result.

Pharaoh's dream. As we move to chapter forty-one, we learn that the Pharaoh has a dream. The narrator does not comment that God caused Pharaoh to dream this dream. (Explicit talk about God is at a minimum in the narrative.) But circumstances lead us to come to the conclusion that this dream is from God.

Pharaoh's dream opens with a peaceful scene of prosperity. Seven well-fed, healthy cows are grazing by the Nile River. However, all of a sudden seven emaciated cows come up out of the river and eat the fat ones! A second dream had a similar pattern. Seven heads of grain on a single stalk were healthy and plump. But then seven wilted ones suddenly appear and consume the healthy ones.

The wise men of Egypt do not have a clue how to interpret these dreams. At this point the cupbearer suddenly remembers his acquaintance back in the prison, Joseph the dream interpreter! Joseph is called in, and he piously exclaims: "It is beyond my power to do this. But God can tell you what it means and set you at ease" (Gen 41:16).

The double dreams mean the same thing. It's likely God used two different dreams with the same message in order to confirm to Pharaoh that the message was indeed intentional. The interpretation, once presented, does not seem all that complex. Seven years of abundance will be followed by seven years of famine.

The knowledge that they had seven years before the arrival of the famine gives Pharaoh time to prepare and to actually turn the disaster into an advantage. In response to Joseph's advice to put the wisest person in Egypt in charge of the preparation, Pharaoh chooses Joseph himself. Pharaoh elevates Joseph to a high position in the land and transforms the Hebrew into an Egyptian. Among other things Joseph takes an Egyptian name (Zaphenath-paneah) and gives him Asenath, the daughter of Potiphera, priest of Heliopolis, as a wife.

During the seven years of plenty Joseph sees that the royal granaries are filled. Then when the famine sets in, the king is in a position to sell grain to those who needed it. Egyptians give not only money but eventually their lands to the Pharaoh in return for the grain, which allows them to survive the famine. This strategy allows the king of Egypt to grow to despotic power. Imagine the effect that this story will have on the generation of the exodus. Through this narrative, they learn that the Pharaoh who oppressed them had such great power only through the intelligence of one of their own ancestors.

Toward the end of chapter forty-one we learn that the famine was not restricted to Egypt but extended outside of its borders. We begin to sense the direction that the narrative is moving, and we aren't surprised that chapter forty-two turns its attention to the plight of Jacob and his extended family back in Canaan.

Reconciliation. Jacob hears about the grain available in Egypt and commands his sons to go there to get food for their survival. The way he speaks to his sons indicates something of a callous attitude toward them, and contrasts with the way he was protective of Joseph and now is protective of Benjamin. He doesn't let Benjamin accompany his brothers to Egypt.

Requests for grain had to go through Joseph, and so the brothers end up making their appeal directly to him. Time and circumstance had changed Joseph, who probably had adopted a thoroughgoing Egyptian style. He recognized them, but they didn't know that the Egyptian governor they were talking to was the brother they sold into slavery. Accordingly, Joseph treats them roughly, questioning them intensely and even accusing them of being spies.

In response to his accusation, they exclaim, "We are honest men, sir! We are not spies!" But though they are not aware of it, this "Egyptian" official has great reason not to trust their integrity, so he devises a test for them. During the interrogation they reveal that there is yet another brother remaining at home, Benjamin. Joseph now demands that they return and come back with this son, thus showing that they were not lying to him. He insists that one of them stay as a hostage till the others return.

Simeon is chosen and the rest return with grain. On the way home the brothers discover that not only do they have the grain but also their money. They don't know how this happened, but since they might be accused of stealing the money, it wasn't considered a good thing.

When they return home and inform Jacob of the situation, their father again shows his favoritism toward Benjamin, the offspring of his beloved Rachel, by refusing to allow Benjamin to go to Egypt, even though the implication was that Simeon would be lost. Simeon had already had a bad reputation with his father (Gen 34; 49:5-7), and Benjamin was just too precious. The brothers try to urge their father to act, Reuben even offers his own two sons as ransom to Jacob, but still the latter refuses. However, when the food they brought back ran out, Jacob relents. Judah makes it clear to his father that they will all die unless they return with Benjamin to Egypt. When he personally guarantees Benjamin's safety, Jacob reluctantly allows them to take Benjamin to Egypt.

When Joseph realizes that his brothers had arrived with Benjamin, he orders his assistant to set up a lunchtime meeting with them. The invitation to eat with Joseph, known to the brothers only as a very powerful Egyptian official, filled them with fear. But when they arrive, they were assured that they were not being brought into his presence on suspicion of stealing the money. Simeon is released and brought to them.

When Joseph arrives for the meal, Benjamin is introduced to him. This introduction proves too much for Joseph; after all this was his full brother. He has to leave the room to control his tears. After Joseph composes himself and returns to the room, the meal begins, and the brothers notice something that is hard for them to explain. The Egyptians are seated at one table, and in keeping with racial prejudices well documented in ancient Egyptian literature, the brothers are seated at a second table. But what amazed them is that they were seated in proper order according to age, and Benjamin was given five times more than any other of them. Certainly this made them wonder what was going on.

However, out of fear, perhaps, they do not inquire, and they take their leave of Joseph to return to Jacob in Canaan. But Joseph has another test in mind. Along with the grain that they requested, he ordered his palace manager to surreptitiously put their money back into the sacks of grain and also place Joseph's own silver cup in Benjamin's sack.

At first we might be tempted to believe this is an act of generosity as before, but he also orders his manager to intercept them on their journey back home and accuse them, and specifically Benjamin, of theft.

What could be the purpose of this strategy? The text doesn't tell us, but it leaves us to infer what Joseph intends. As we reflect on the shape of the story, we see that Joseph has created as closely as he could a situation similar to his own. Joseph had been; now Benjamin is clearly the newly favored son of Jacob. This raises the question, Will the other brothers sell out their half-brother to save themselves?

The answer comes quickly. No. The brothers are willing to sacrifice themselves for Benjamin and the well-being of their father Jacob. In particular, Judah, who we have seen has not always acted with the highest integrity (see Gen 38), offers to take the punishment in the place of Benjamin.

Joseph now has his answer. He reveals his identity to his brothers. They are dumbfounded, but Joseph shows awareness already that his suffering is not without meaning. "It was God who sent me here ahead of you to preserve your lives. . . . God has sent me ahead of you to keep you and your families alive and to preserve many survivors. So it was God who sent me here, not you!" (Gen 45:5, 7-8). A family reunited and rescued from a severe famine!

Jacob is told the wonderful news, and along with his extended family of approximately seventy people, he moves to Egypt, at Pharaoh's invitation, to weather the famine. As events unfold, the family stays in Egypt for many years, even centuries. But for now Jacob is happy at the reunion and with the promise of abundance during a lengthy famine.

Jacob's last words. Before he dies, we hear his final words, in essence his last will and testament, directed to his descendants. First, in Genesis 48 the patriarch blesses both of Joseph's children, Manasseh and Ephraim. Surprisingly, and to Joseph's chagrin, his father blesses the latter, who is younger, over the former. Joseph at first thinks his father has made an error, but that is not the case. As in Jacob's own situation the younger receives the blessing of the right hand, though in this case both children receive different gradations of blessing. The blessing of Joseph's children indicate that Joseph will receive a kind of double blessing in relationship to his brothers. The sons of Jacob, now called Israel, are the fathers of the tribes of Israel. When the dust settles years later (at the time of Joshua), we see that the tribes of Manasseh and Ephraim, not a single tribe of Joseph, receive land along with Joseph's brothers.

Even so, Genesis 49 offers Jacob's blessings and curses on his twelve sons, and these are indeed portents of future events and relationships. He begins with Leah's children. Reuben is the oldest, and he would expect to receive a great blessing. However, Reuben had spoiled his relationship with his father by sleeping with his concubine Bilhah (Gen 35:22). By such a shameful act, he lost his status as firstborn. The tribe of Reuben will have no distinctive position in the future of Israel.

We might think that the same fate awaited both Simeon and Levi, because they too shamed their father by their massacre of the Shechemites (see pp. 145-47). Jacob now curses these two sons of Leah to dispersion through the land of Israel. And indeed, both tribes fail to receive a tribal allotment in the second half of the book of Joshua. The fate of Simeon is to be absorbed into the larger tribe of Judah, receiving some cities within that tribe's boundaries. Levi, on the other hand, though dispersed, arguably becomes the most distinctive of all tribes. They are the priestly tribe. The difference? They come to Moses' aid out of loyalty to Yahweh and avenge the rebellion of their fellow Israelites who worship the golden calf (Ex 32—34).[1]

Judah is the first to receive a blessing from his father, and it is quite a blessing. The promise of leadership is given to Judah. It is from his tribe that "the scepter (a royal symbol) will not depart." Though the first king is a Benjaminite (Saul), it is to a Judean, David, that the promise of a dynasty is given (2 Sam 7), and from this line the Messiah will come.

Jacob also says positive things about Zebulun and Issachar, but certainly nothing on the scale of what has just been said to Judah. The same can be said of the tribes that descend from the children of the concubines, Bilhah and Zilpah: Dan, Gad, Asher and Naphtali.

The final blessings come on the sons of Rachel, Joseph and Benjamin. As might be expected, the longest is for the former, and in it Jacob speaks of great prosperity. Benjamin's blessing also seems positive, but it concerns success in warfare.

After imparting these last words the narrative tells us that Jacob dies. In accordance with his wishes, he is not buried in Egypt, but rather taken to Canaan, where he is placed in the tomb near Hebron that Abraham bought years before when Sarah died. This certainly is a reminder that though temporary happiness and survival has been found in Egypt, it is not their land, the land of promise.

We are now in a better position to understand the import of the words that Joseph delivers at the end of his story, though we stated them at the beginning of our retelling. The brothers intended evil toward Joseph, but God turned it to good. Potiphar's wife acted with evil intent toward Joseph, but God turned it to good. The chief cupbearer did not act righteously toward Joseph, but God created the circumstances that brought Joseph into Pharaoh's presence.

What is this good that God worked toward? The survival of the people of promise. The covenant would not fail.

To the future. The book of Genesis ends happily, then, but without a strong sense of closure. True, the conclusion of the book is marked by the end of Joseph's life. But in the narration of his death, we get a strong sense of narrative pause, not finality. The book ends with Joseph's request:

"When God comes to help you and lead you back, you must take my bones with you" (Gen 50:25). So the curtain closes, not at the end of the play but only between the first two episodes. The story will continue in the book of Exodus.

God's blessing has not yet been fully restored, but at the end of the book of Genesis, we see that God's blessing of a single individual led to the blessing of an entire family. The book ends with the twelve sons of Israel looking into the future. These twelve sons are the forebears to the twelve tribes of Israel (see Gen 49), and thus we can see how Genesis, though a family story, is a preamble to a national history.

P A R T

READING GENESIS
AS CHRISTIANS

■   ■   ■

In this final chapter we turn to a Christian reading of the book of Genesis. To many, including many Christians, the idea of a "Christian reading" is preposterous and distorting. They would argue that we must guard against importing later ideas and developments back into the ancient Israelite text.

Indeed, such warnings need to be heard because some tremendously fanciful interpretations have been presented by those who see Christ hidden away in the pages of the Old Testament. So we must be careful as we talk about Christ in the book of Genesis. However, as mentioned in chapter two, Jesus himself encourages his followers to expect to read about him in the pages of the Old Testament (Lk 24:22-27, 44-48).

In what follows I am not claiming that the human author(s) of Genesis had a detailed awareness of how his words would play out in the history of redemption. However, we have already expressed our understanding that there is an ultimate Author standing behind the human author. We couldn't presume to know the Author's intentions if it weren't for the New Testament. Later revelation brings out the fuller significance of these ancient words, and it's from the perspective of the New Testament that we now read the book of Genesis.

We should be clear about what I am doing in the following section. I am presenting examples of a christological reading of Genesis. I make no attempt to be exhaustive. Nor am I concerned with a broader New Testament appropriation of the Old Testament.

My concern is focused because I believe that this is a crucial element of Old Testament interpretation missing from much Old Testament reading and preaching, to the detriment of the church. The lack of an appreciation of the christological dimension leads to a diminishment of preaching from the Old Testament. Or when it is preached, it is frequently only moralistic. Certainly the Old Testament should be preached and read for its ethical lessons, but there is more to it than that, and the "more" is what Jesus is pointing us toward in Luke 24.

TEN

THE CHRISTOLOGICAL DIFFERENCE

Whether we accept Moses as the author of Genesis or not, we all recognize that it was written and finally edited well before the time of Jesus Christ. However, the authors of the New Testament understand that its message has relevance to the gospel of Jesus Christ, demonstrated by quoting from Genesis time and again.

Jesus himself invited, even required, his disciples to read the whole Old Testament in the light of his coming suffering and glorification. The New Testament authors apparently did this (Lk 24), and we should do so as well.

The interpretations of Genesis that are found in the New Testament were not necessarily those that would have occurred to the original audience or the author(s) of the Old Testament book. They may have had a sense that the message had a meaning that would stretch beyond what they consciously knew, but it took the event itself to illumine the depths of the meaning of the book of Genesis. Once Christ came, his followers realized the full significance of the book.

This doesn't mean that New Testament authors or modern readers can impose a meaning on the text. The christological meaning is not something external to the text itself. It is derived from the text. There isn't a secret meaning or a code that we need a key to decipher. Proper christological readings of the Old Testament are not forced or arbitrary.

While it would be quite impossible to be exhaustive in our christological reading of Genesis, we can be suggestive. We will take four important texts and explore how the New Testament treats them in relationship to Jesus Christ. We will begin with the so-called protoevangelium, then move on to the promise of a seed or descendants given to Abraham, the story of Melchizedek and finally consider Joseph as a character who anticipates Jesus.

GENESIS 3:15: THE PROTOEVANGELIUM

From now on, you and the woman will be enemies, and your offspring and her offspring will be enemies. He will crush your head, and you will strike his heel.

The literary context. Genesis 3:15 is part of the curse against the serpent. The first two chapters of Genesis are an account of the creation of the cosmos and of human beings. In these chapters Adam and Eve enjoy an intimate relationship with God and each other in the Garden of Eden. Genesis 2 ends on a note of peace and harmony.[1]

In Genesis 3 the serpent appears, and he deceives the woman who eats from the forbidden tree of the knowledge of good and evil. Adam, her husband, who was with her during her dialogue with the serpent, eats without offering any resistance. At this point God intervenes and punishes each of the three players in the rebellion. He begins with the serpent, and Genesis 3:15 belongs to this section of the story.

How would the New Testament authors have understood Genesis 3:15 in the aftermath of Christ's death and resurrection?

Reading the verse in its ancient context. If we imagine ourselves hearing this story at the time of Moses (not to speak of the time frame in which the story is set), we must admit that the identity of the serpent is somewhat mystifying. All we have learned in the narrative thus far is that God has created everything, including all creatures, and pronounced it "good." Up to this point in the narrative we have absolutely no indication of anything being amiss.

Where in the world did this "shrewdest of all the wild animals" (Gen 3:1) come from? And how can the serpent be so obviously evil, speaking contrary to his Maker and seducing God's human creatures to join him in what appears to be rebellion? The narrative doesn't explain, and the attempts on the part of some Bible readers to fit a fall of angels into the "gap" between the first two verses of Genesis 1 shows how desperate people are to come up with an explanation. Indeed, nowhere in the Bible is there an explanation of how evil was first introduced into the cosmos. While space does not permit a rebuttal, arguments presented on the basis of Isaiah 14 and Ezekiel 28 are not credible.[2] The serpent simply appears with no explanation of its origin.

In addition, the curse against the serpent is tantalizingly ambiguous when read in its ancient context. How would someone during the Old Testament time period understand the reference to "your [the serpent's] offspring" and "her [the woman's] offspring"? It's extremely doubtful that Genesis 3:15 would have been read in a messianic sense during the Old Testament time period. Certainly such a reading cannot be proven. The fact that the text is not picked up and developed in later canonical books is a good indication of this truth.

Within the context of the chapters that follow, a strong case can be made for the idea that the seed of the woman refers to those human descendants who are on the side of God (cf. the Sethite genealogy of Gen 5), and the seed of the serpent to those who resist God (cf. the Cainite genealogy of Gen 4:17-26).

Nevertheless, it's also clear that the New Testament authors, who are reading Genesis after Christ, understood Genesis 3:15 to have a more profound and ultimate meaning. No doubt attends the fact that the early church identified the serpent with Satan and Jesus Christ as the "seed of the woman."

At the end of the book of Romans, Paul encourages his readers with: "The God of peace will soon crush Satan under your feet. May the grace of our Lord Jesus Christ be with you" (Rom 16:20). Paul here clearly identifies Satan with the serpent. After all, Satan will be crushed underfoot. The agent of Satan's destruction, however, is the church, with whom

Christ is said to be present. Though the people of God will be the agent of Satan's demise, it is the God of peace who will be the force behind the people's victory.

A second passage, Hebrews 2:14-15, is less clearly citing Genesis 3:15, but many[3] make the argument that there is an allusion to it:

Because God's children are human beings—made of flesh and blood—the Son also became flesh and blood. For only as a human being could he die, and only by dying could he break the power of the devil, who had the power of death. Only in this way could he set free all who have lived their lives as slaves to the fear of dying.

This passage speaks of Jesus breaking the power of the devil by dying, and so the necessity of his taking a human form. Perhaps it is in this way that Paul in the earlier passage believes that the God of peace crushed Satan under the feet of human beings.

The third place where we find language associated with Genesis 3:15 and applied to Satan and Christ is found in the book of Revelation:

Then there was war in heaven. Michael and his angels fought against the dragon and his angels. And the dragon lost the battle, and he and his angels were forced out of heaven. This great dragon—the ancient serpent called the devil, or Satan, the one deceiving the whole world—was thrown down to the earth with all his angels. (Rev 12:7-9)

Here the connection with Genesis 3:15 is also obvious. Satan is called the "ancient serpent," an unmistakable allusion to our text under consideration.

In summary, then, the early church read the Old Testament story in Genesis 3 and could not help but see the serpent associated with Satan, now more fully understood based on later revelation. It also understood that that crushing of Satan was now underway in connection with Christ's victory over him on the cross.

Is this a fair way of reading the text? Indeed, it would be hard to see how the church after Jesus could read it any other way. By the time of the New Testament authors, Satan is a much further developed character in the Bible. God progressively reveals his truth to his people, and in the later Old Testament and certainly in the New Testament period the people of God had come to know the personal nature of evil much more profoundly. Going back to Genesis 3 it is hard to miss the character of Satan in the serpent. Once that connection is made, it would be even more difficult to miss the connection between Jesus and the seed of the woman. The woman here is Eve, and Jesus, fully human as well as fully divine, is a "son of Eve." In Jesus' crucifixion Satan bruises his heel; he brings harm to Jesus, but it does not completely do Jesus in; God raises him from death. Thanks to the resurrection the church understood this as the defeat of Satan. Granted this defeat is an already-but-not-yet act, since Satan and evil are not extinguished until the second coming (Rev 20:7-10), but that victory is certain.

Thus Christian readers can go back to Genesis 3 and read the first announcement of the good news (the evangelium) there. It's best to acknowledge that the first readers may not have recognized this, but that the ultimate author's purposes are recognized by the New Testament authors as they read the Old Testament in the light of the person and work of Jesus Christ.

Before leaving this topic, though, we must consider one more factor. While the New Testament is the first to connect Genesis 3:15 with the work of Jesus, it is not the first to identify the serpent with Satan or the agent of destruction with the Messiah. For that we can turn to Jewish literature that comes from the period between the Testaments.

GENESIS 12:1-3: ABRAHAM'S SEED

In Genesis 12 God promises Abraham that he will "make you into a great nation" (v. 2). This promise entails both land and descendants. And in terms of descendants the promise is often explicated along the lines found in Genesis 15:5: "Then the LORD took Abram outside and said to him, 'Look up into the sky and count the stars if you can. That's how many descendants you will have.'" In other words, the fulfillment of this promise is clearly associated with the multiplication of Abraham's descendants, later known as the Israelites. Thus it is surprising to find Paul making the following argument in Galatians 3:15-16:

Dear brothers and sisters, here's an example from everyday life. Just as no one
can set aside or amend an irrevocable agreement, so it is in this case. God gave
the promises to Abraham and his child. And notice that the Scripture doesn't say
"to his children," as if it meant many descendants. Rather, it says "to his
child"—and that, of course, means Christ.

And that, of course, means Christ! Really?

Paul knew the Old Testament deeply and profoundly. We know that
since he is described in Acts 22:3 as a student of the renowned rabbi Ga-
maliel, at whose feet he was "carefully trained in our Jewish laws and customs." He certainly knew and affirmed that the Hebrew Scriptures stated
that the Abrahamic promise was realized in the children of Israel.

Nevertheless, Paul is reading the Old Testament in the light of the
Christ event and sees an even more important fulfillment of the covenant
promise in Jesus himself. And, in keeping with rather common first-cen-
tury exegetical practice, he exploits the fact that the term *descendant* or
seed in Genesis 12 is a collective singular. And in the context of a broader
argument in Galatians 3 as a whole that law (the Mosaic covenant) does
not trump faith (the Abrahamic covenant), Paul asserts that the Abrahamic promise finds its ultimate fulfillment in Christ.

Thus today when Christians read Genesis 12:1-3, while affirming its Old
Testament fulfillment in Abraham's biological descendants, the most important realization is in Christ. In this way Christians find themselves involved in the Abrahamic promise of a seed, because according to Galatians
3:29, "Now that you belong to Christ, you are the true children of Abraham. You are his heirs, and God's promise to Abraham belongs to you."

GENESIS 14:17-20: MELCHIZEDEK

According to the book of Hebrews, Jesus is a priest in the line of
Melchizedek. Indeed, two extensive passages develop this idea (Heb
4:14—5:10; 7:1—9:13), but the basic idea is expressed in the following
verses:

In this way, God qualified him as a perfect High Priest, and he became the
source of eternal salvation for all those who obey him. And God designated him

to be a High Priest in the order of Melchizedek. (Heb 5:9-10)

Our attention is drawn to these references connecting Christ and Melchizedek since we first encounter the latter in an enigmatic passage in Genesis 14:

> *After Abram returned from his victory over Kedorlaomer and his allies, the king of Sodom came out to meet him in the valley of Shaveh (that is, the King's Valley). And Melchizedek, the king of Salem and a priest of God Most High, brought Abram some bread and wine. Melchizedek blessed Abram with this blessing:*

> *Blessed be Abram by God Most High,*
> *Creator of heaven and earth.*
> *And blessed be God Most High,*
> *who has defeated your enemies for you.*

> *Then Abram gave Melchizedek a tenth of all the goods he had recovered. (Gen 14:17-20)*

The context. The story of Abraham's meeting with Melchizedek is found in the context of the Abraham narrative, but it strikes us as an interruption of the main theme of Genesis 12—26. The main theme concerns the divine promise that God will make a great nation out of Abraham's descendants, and the focus of the narrative is on the first step in the fulfillment of these promises, namely, the birth of a child to Abraham and Sarah. The latter proves to be barren and so the fulfillment of the promise appears to be threatened. The story of Abraham in the main concerns the patriarch's reaction to the obstacles to fulfillment (see pp. 129-36 for a fuller explication).

Genesis 14 appears to have a different function. The chapter begins with the description of an incursion of four kings from outside the land of Canaan against five kings, presumably in Canaan, headed by the kings of Sodom and Gomorrah. The five kings of Canaan had been subject to King Kedorlaomer, the head of the other coalition, for a number of years. Kedorlaomer's coalition was reacting to a rebellion and came to bring their vassals back into line. In the process they defeated other tribes, some of which have significant reputations as warriors (the Rephaites, the Zuzites, the Emites, the Horites, the whole territory of Amalekites and Amorites). When the five kings met Kedorlaomer's coalition, they were scattered, and in the process Lot, Abraham's nephew who had moved to the vicinity of Sodom and Gomorrah (Gen 13), was captured.

Abraham soon was informed of this disaster, and he set out with 318 men and defeated the coalition of foreign kings, recovering not only Lot but also the other plunder that the kings had taken from the Canaanite coalition. It was on his return that Abraham had his meeting with Melchizedek. After paying homage to Melchizedek, Abraham distances himself from the other kings of the land by refusing to take any of the plunder for himself.

New Testament connections. Why does the book of Hebrews associate Jesus with Melchizedek, and what is the significance of this connection? A popular understanding of the relationship is that Melchizedek is an Old Testament christophany; that is, Melchizedek is Jesus. But, on the contrary, I suggest that the connection with Jesus results because of the enigmatic nature of Melchizedek's appearance in the narrative as well as some of the details of his description.

Melchizedek appears suddenly and unexpectedly, with little explanation. When we read this story, we come away with the question of this person's identity. What is Abraham doing recognizing a Canaanite priest-king as a co-religionist? Even more, we stand amazed at the fact that Abraham honors Melchizedek as a superior by presenting him with the tithe of the plunder. Furthermore, his very name resonates with significance even if we can't be dogmatic about the details. That is, it is made up of two elements: "king" (*melekh*) and "righteous" (*tsedeq*). Questions remain as to whether his name means "my king is righteous" or "the king of righteousness." It is also unclear whether one of the two parts should be understand as a divine name or epithet. A further uncertainty concerns the place where the action takes place. It is given the name Salem in parallel with Zion, which strongly suggests Jerusalem,[4] but others think it is connected with the word *peace* and may point to another location.

It seems to me that the author of Hebrews, reading the Old Testament in the light of the Christ event, exploits the ambiguity of the story in order to make important theological claims about Jesus.

However, before proceeding directly to the book of Hebrews, it's important to note the only other place in the Bible where Melchizedek is mentioned: Psalm 110. Psalm 110, understood in its Old Testament context, is a royal psalm, appropriate especially for the inauguration of a Davidic king. The first verse cites Yahweh, "the LORD," as telling "my Lord" (the human king) to sit at God's right hand while he defeats his enemies. Here we should note the similarity with that other great psalm of royal inauguration, Psalm 2.

Psalm 2 pronounces a divine blessing on the Davidic king and predicts his success and victory. This psalm also has a relationship with the establishment of the Davidic covenant in 2 Samuel 7. In the context of this psalm the Davidic king is proclaimed a priest in the order of Melchizedek (v. 4). Of course, the Israelite king could not function as an Aaronic priest, since the latter are Levites. But Melchizedek is a more appropriate connection because he was a king-priest who ruled in the city of Salem—(Jeru)salem.

However, the history of the descendants of David is not a happy one. Rarely after David did these kings serve the Lord with exclusive commitment and passion (Hezekiah and Josiah most notable among the exceptions). Toward the end of the Old Testament period, it became clear that these texts awaited association with a future ideal messianic king, and the New Testament authors then recognized that Jesus was the long-awaited Messiah.

This is how the author of the book Hebrews reads Genesis 14 and Psalm 110, and recognizes Jesus. It's wrong to think of Melchizedek as a preincarnate appearance of Jesus. It's equally wrong to think of these texts as messianic prophecies whose sole purpose is to foreshadow the coming of Jesus. Rather, when the author of Hebrews wanted to talk about Jesus being the ultimate priest, one who surpasses even Aaron, the enigmatic story of Melchizedek was a means of expressing that truth. After all, as Abraham honored Melchizedek, Levi "was in Abraham's body" (Heb 7:10), and thus not only Aaron but all Levites were symbolically acknowledging the superiority of Melchizedek. Furthermore, since Psalm 110 suggests a combination of the roles of the priest and the warrior king, the author of Hebrews understood that Jesus was the most perfect expression of these roles, even surpassing the Davidic king who was the most immediate referent of this poem. Indeed, in its Old Testament context its most likely setting is as a coronation hymn. The latter connection is particularly understandable considering the relationship between David and Jesus, who is frequently described as David's son (e.g., Mt 1:1; 9:27; 12:23; 22:43, 45 [citing Ps 110]; Rom 1:3; 2 Tim 2:8) with the intention of showing that he is the fulfillment of the Davidic covenant, which stated that a son of David will rule forever (2 Sam 7).

Surely the original readers, and probably the writer of Genesis 14, would not have anticipated how the author of Hebrews would use the narrative concerning Melchizedek. However, in the light of the experience of Jesus Christ, the inspired author of Hebrews could not help but recognize the connection.[5] But is there a greater priest or greater warrior-king than Jesus?

GENESIS 37—50: JOSEPH AND JESUS

Finally, we come to the story of Joseph. Nowhere is Joseph connected with Jesus in the New Testament. Certainly, there is nothing like prophecy in the narrative account of the life of Joseph. However, reading the story of Joseph in the light of the gospel leads the sensitive reader to note an analogy between the way God worked salvation through the life of Joseph and how he did so climactically in the life of Jesus. Joseph was God's agent in the rescue of the family of God. Jacob and his family, the seed of Abraham, survived the famine because Joseph was in a position to supply them with grain. Why was he there? Because of a series of wicked acts on the part of his brothers and others. In Joseph's words, "You intended to harm me, but God intended it all for good. He brought me to this position so I could save the lives of many people" (Gen 50:20). God used the evil deeds of others to bring about the survival of his people.

We hear a similar theme in Peter's reflection on the death of Christ in Acts 2:22-24:

> *People of Israel, listen! God publicly endorsed Jesus of Nazareth by doing pow-*

erful miracles, wonders, and signs through him, as you well know. But God knew what would happen, and his prearranged plan was carried out when Jesus was betrayed. With the help of lawless Gentiles, you nailed him to a cross and killed him. But God released him from the horrors of death and raised him back to life, for death could not keep him in its grip.

As the Roman soldiers were nailing Christ's hands to the cross, they were fulfilling God's plan of redemption. What they meant for evil, God meant for the salvation of the world.

CONCLUSION

In this chapter we have followed the instructions of none other than Jesus himself who in Luke 24 taught his disciples to read the Old Testament in the light of his coming. I have chosen a few representative texts in order to reveal how we should be sensitive to the flow of redemptive history that climaxes in Jesus as we read the ancient text of Genesis.

Interpretive principle. After reading Genesis as if we are part of the original audience, we should then read the book in the full knowledge of the redemptive history that follows, particularly the death and resurrection of Christ. In this the New Testament authors' use of the Genesis material should shape our thinking.

COMMENTARIES ON THE
BOOK OF GENESIS

All of the following commentaries are excellent; which one you should purchase depends on what you are looking for; not every commentary can address every aspect of the book, and the various commentaries come from different theological and methodological perspectives.

Aalders, G. Charles. *Genesis.* 2 vols. Bible Student's Commentary. Grand Rapids: Zondervan, 1981. This is an English translation of a commentary originally published in Dutch in 1949. Although somewhat dated, Aalder's work retains its value as a theological commentary. Writing from within the Reformed tradition, Aalders shows great exegetical skill and theological insight.

Brueggemann, Walter. *Genesis.* Interpretation. Atlanta: John Knox Press, 1982. Brueggemann, although a moderately critical scholar, is always stimulating and insightful. His commentary concentrates on the final form of the text and focuses principally on the theology of the book.

Cassuto, Umberto. *From Adam to Abraham: A Commentary on the Book of Genesis.* Translated by I. Abrahams. 2 vols. Jerusalem: Magnes Press, 1964. This is an excellent commentary on the first eleven chapters of

Genesis. Cassuto, a conservative Jewish writer, died unexpectedly before the book was completed. He was a brilliant philologist and literary scholar. He, interestingly, goes against the scholarly tide and rejects the documentary hypothesis.

Hamilton, Victor P. *The Book of Genesis*. 2 vols. New International Commentary on the Old Testament. Grand Rapids: Eerdmans, 1990, 1995. Hamilton does an excellent job interpreting the text in a positive way as well as handling the difficult questions of the book (creation story, history of patriarchs, religion of patriarchs). Between Wenham and Hamilton, Genesis is well covered.

Hartley, John E. *Genesis*. New International Biblical Commentary: Old Testament. Peabody, Mass.: Hendrickson, 2000. I can't always agree with Hartley's analysis of the structure of the book of Genesis or with his analysis of sections of it as a palistrophe (the arrangement of material in a V-shaped pattern, also known as chiasm), but Hartley nonetheless offers a clear and straightforward analysis of Genesis. The depth of exposition is constrained by the series. His arguments in favor of Mosaic involvement in the production of the book and also in favor of the patriarchal narratives is refreshing.

Ross, Allen P. *Creation and Blessing: A Guide to the Study and Exposition of Genesis*. Grand Rapids: Baker, 1988. The book opens with a short introduction to the author's method of approach to Genesis. Ross presents an evangelical alternative to the documentary approach. The bulk of his treatment, however, is more like a running exposition with an emphasis on theology. As such it is often insightful and helpful. A good book, especially for pastors preaching through the book of Genesis.

Sarna, Nahum M. *Genesis*. JPS Torah Commentary. Philadelphia: Jewish Publication Society, 1989. This commentary is a verse-by-verse, virtually word-by-word, study. Although Sarna recognizes the composite nature of Genesis, he treats the book as a whole in the commentary. Though he deals with other aspects of the text, his emphasis is on Near Eastern background and Jewish tradition.

Waltke, Bruce K., and Cathi J. Fredricks. *Genesis*. Grand Rapids: Zondervan, 2001. This commentary is not in a series but is well worth tracking down and adding to a reference library. Waltke is the dean of evangelical biblical studies, and this commentary is exegetically insightful and theologically rich.

Walton, John H. *Genesis*. New International Version Application Commentary. Grand Rapids: Zondervan, 2001. Walton's commentary is stimulating and well-written. He navigates the difficult issues of the book well. Unfortunately, he rarely comments on the relationship between Genesis and the New Testament.

Wenham, Gordon J. *Genesis 1—15* and *Genesis 16—50*. Word Biblical Commentary. Waco, Tex.: Word, 1987, 1994. Wenham is one of the finest evangelical commentators today. His commentary on Genesis shows his high level of scholarship and his exegetical sensitivity. He represents a conservative approach to Genesis, but he doesn't completely reject source theory.

NOTES

Preface

[1]Tremper Longman III, *How to Read the Psalms* (Downers Grove, Ill.: InterVarsity Press, 1988), and *How to Read Proverbs* (Downers Grove, Ill.: InterVarsity Press, 2002).

[2]John H. Walton's *Genesis,* New International Version Application Commentary (Grand Rapids: Zondervan, 2001) is particularly insightful when it comes to the theme of the blessing in the book of Genesis.

Part I: Reading Genesis with a Strategy

[1]Tremper Longman III, *How to Read the Psalms* (Downers Grove, Ill.: InterVarsity Press, 1988), and *How to Read Proverbs* (Downers Grove, Ill.: InterVarsity Press, 2002).

Chapter 1: Understanding the Book of "Beginnings"

[1]For a good introduction to these issues, consult Tremper Longman III, *Reading the Bible with Heart and Mind* (Colorado Springs, Colo.: NavPress, 1997); Gordon D. Fee and Douglas Stuart, *How to Read the Bible for All Its Worth,* 3rd ed. (Grand Rapids: Zondervan, 2003).

[2]Tremper Longman III, *Literary Approaches to Biblical Interpretation* (Grand Rapids: Zondervan, 1987), pp. 63-71, and "Literary Approaches to Old Testament Study," in *The Face of Old Testament Studies,* ed. David W. Baker and Bill T. Arnold (Grand Rapids: Baker, 1999), pp. 97-115.

[3]The Hebrew spoken in Israel today, though built from biblical Hebrew, is substantially different in grammar and vocabulary.

[4]We will discuss later whether Genesis was written at a single moment or over a long period of time and by more than one author (see pp. 41-53).

[5]Robert Alter, "How Convention Helps Us to Read: The Case of the Bible's Annunciation Type Scene," *Prooftexts* 3 (1983): 115.

[6]Herman Ridderbos (*Redemptive History and the New Testament Scriptures,* 2nd ed. [Phillipsburg, N.J.: Presbyterian & Reformed, 1988]) remains the best study concerning the

theological foundation of canon, though Roger T. Beckwith (*The Old Testament Canon of the New Testament Church* [London: SPCK, 1985]) is clearly the fullest presentation of the history of the church's attestation.

[7]For recent discussions, see the provocative work of Walter Brueggemann, *Theology of the Old Testament* (Minneapolis: Fortress, 1997), and John Goldingay, *Old Testament Theology: Israel's Gospel* (Downers Grove, Ill.: InterVarsity Press, 2003).

[8]According to 1 Pet 1:10-12, the prophets spoke better than they knew.

[9]See the list and evaluation of Genesis commentaries provided in the appendix.

Chapter 2: Who Wrote Genesis?

[1]For explanations of D and P see pp. 52-53.

[2]Harold Bloom and David Rosenberg, *The Book of J* (New York: Vintage, 1991).

[3]For a representative of those in favor of this position, see J. Alberto Soggin, *Introduction to the Old Testament* (Philadelphia: Westminster Press, 1976), p. 107. A representative of those skeptical of this position is Otto Eissfeldt, *The Old Testament: An Introduction* (New York: Harper & Row, 1965), p. 203.

[4]*Linchpin* is Gordon Wenham's, found in his "The Date of Deuteronomy: Linchpin of Old Testament Criticism: Part II," *Themelios* 11 (1985): 15-17.

[5]Eissfeldt, *Old Testament*, p. 208.

[6]See, for example, Umberto Cassuto, *The Documentary Hypothesis*, trans. I. Abrahams (Jerusalem: Magnes Press, 1961 [Hebrew ed., 1941]); Edward J. Young, *An Introduction to the Old Testament* (Grand Rapids: Eerdmans, 1949); Oswald T. Allis, *The Five Books of Moses* (Phillipsburg, N.J.: Presbyterian & Reformed, 1943).

[7]R. Norman Whybray, *The Making of the Pentateuch: A Methodological Study*, JSOTS 53 (Sheffield, U.K.: JSOT Press, 1987); Isaac M. Kikawada and Arthur Quinn, *Before Abraham Was: The Unity of Genesis 1-11* (Nashville: Abingdon, 1985); Gordon Wenham, *Genesis*, 2 vols. (Waco, Tex.: Word, 1987, 1994); Kenneth A. Kitchen, *Ancient Orient and the Old Testament* (Downers Grove, Ill.: InterVarsity Press, 1967), and *On the Reliability of the Old Testament* (Grand Rapids: Eerdmans, 2003).

[8]E. A. Speiser, *Genesis* (Garden City, N.Y.: Doubleday, 1964), p. 91.

[9]Robert Alter, *The Art of Biblical Narrative* (New York: Basic Books, 1981), pp. 47-62.

[10]See the discussion in Iain Provan, V. Philips Long and Tremper Longman III, *A Biblical History of Israel* (Louisville: Westminster John Knox, 2003), p. 122, and E. Fry, "How Was Joseph Taken to Egypt? (Genesis 37:12-36)," *The Bible Translator* 46 (1995): 446.

[11]J. Gordon McConville provides a different understanding of the relationship between Deuteronomy 12 and Exodus 20, but he similarly moves away from a source explanation (*Law and Theology in Deuteronomy*, JSOTS 33 [Sheffield, U.K.: JSOT Press, 1984]).

[12]T. Desmond Alexander, *Abraham in the Negev: A Source-Critical Investigation of Genesis 20:1—22:19* (Carlisle, U.K.: Paternoster, 1997), and "Authorship," in *Dictionary of the Old Testament: Pentateuch*, ed. T. Desmond Alexander and David W. Baker (Downers Grove, Ill.: InterVarsity Press, 2003), pp. 61-72.

Chapter 3: The Shape of the Book of Genesis

[1]G. N. Leech and M. H. Short, *Style in Fiction* (London: Longman, 1981), pp. 19, 74.

[2]A survey of critical approaches to this question regarding Genesis may be found in John Van Seters, *Prologue to History: The Yahwist as Historian in Genesis* (Louisville: Westminster John Knox, 1992), pp. 10-23.

[3]Hermann Gunkel, cited in George W. Coats, *Genesis with an Introduction to Narrative Literature*, Forms of the Old Testament Literature 1 (Grand Rapids: Eerdmans, 1983), p. 319.

[4]Walter Moberly, *At the Mountain of God: Story and Theology in Exodus 32—34* (Sheffield, U.K.: JSOT Press, 1983).

[5]David M. Howard Jr., *An Introduction to the Old Testament Historical Books* (Chicago: Moody Press, 1993), pp. 30, 35.

[6]V. Philips Long, "Narrative and History: Stories about the Past," in Iain Provan, V. Philips Long and Tremper Longman III, *A Biblical History of Israel* (Louisville: Westminster John Knox, 2003), p. 82; see also pp. 84-87.

[7]Walter Brueggemann, *Genesis* (Atlanta: John Knox Press, 1982), p. 105.

[8]For a historical perspective on the literary study of the Bible, see the concise discussion in Tremper Longman III, "Literary Approaches to Old Testament Study," in *The Face of Old Testament Studies*, ed. David W. Baker and Bill T. Arnold (Grand Rapids: Baker, 1999), pp. 97-115.

[9]A sampling includes John H. Sailhamer, "Genesis," in *A Complete Literary Guide to the Bible*, ed. Lee Ryken and Tremper Longman III (Grand Rapids: Zondervan, 1995), pp. 108-20; Robert Alter, *The Art of Biblical Narrative* (New York: Basic Books, 1981); J. P. Fokkelman, *Narrative Art in Genesis* (Amsterdam: Van Gorcum, 1975). More recently, Paul Borgman, *Genesis: The Story We Haven't Heard* (Downers Grove, Ill.: InterVarsity Press, 2001). The latter is very good, but the subtitle is misleading and somewhat self-promoting. He's hardly the first to study the book of Genesis in this way.

[10]David Rhoads and Donald Michie, *Mark as Story: The Introduction to the Narrative of a Gospel* (Philadelphia: Fortress, 1982), pp. 3-4.

[11]Bruce K. Waltke, "Was Cain's Offering Rejected by God Because It Was Not a Blood Sacrifice?" *Westminster Theological Journal* 48 (1986): 363-72.

[12]Ibid., p. 369.

Chapter 4: Myth or History?

[1]Jacobus van Dijk, "Myth and Mythmaking in Ancient Egypt," in *Civilizations of the Ancient Near East,* ed. Jack M. Sasson (New York: Scribner's, 1995), 3:1697-98.

[2]For a helpful synthesis of Egyptian cosmogonic ideas, see John D. Currid, *Ancient Egypt and the Old Testament* (Grand Rapids: Baker, 1997), pp. 53-73.

[3]Egyptian accounts use different metaphors to describe the process of emanation of the other deities from the creator god. Two of the most prominent are sneezing and masturbating.

[4]See *The Context of Scripture,* ed. William W. Hallo and K. Lawson Younger Jr. (Boston: Brill, 1997), 1:21-22.

[5]Ibid., p. 22.

[6]According to W. G. Lambert ("Kosmogonie," in *Reallexikon fer Assyriologie* [Berlin/ Leipzig: deGruyter, 1990], 6:218-22), Mesopotamia actually is more interested in theogony than cosmogony. Of course, the two are integrally related, since the gods represent aspects of the created order.

[7]The translation of Benjamin R. Foster, *The Context of Scripture* (Leiden: Brill, 1997), 1:398.

[8]W. G. Lambert and A. R. Millard, *Atra-Hasis: The Babylonian Story of the Flood* (Oxford: Clarendon Press, 1969). See also Alan R. Millard, "A New Babylonian 'Genesis' Story," *Tyndale Bulletin* 18 (1967): 3-18.

[9]Benjamin R. Foster, *Before the Muses* (Bethesda, Md.: CDL Press, 1993), 1:165.

[10]See Thorkild Jacobsen, "The Battle between Marduk and Tiamat," *Journal of American Oriental Society* 88 (1968): 104-8.

[11]Of course, there are differences among the different Near Eastern texts, and even within the accounts of the various regions of the Near East, but for the purposes of this chapter we will focus on the similarities and differences between Genesis and the ancient Near Eastern texts as a group.

[12]Samuel N. Kramer, *The Sumerians* (Chicago: University of Chicago Press, 1963), p. 149.

[13]Howard N. Wallace emphasizes that both Mesopotamian and the biblical text ascribe labor as the purpose of the creation of humanity; however, he errs in not pointing out the difference in terms of the quality of the work and relationship with the divine realm (*The Eden Narrative* [Atlanta: Scholars Press, 1985], p. 70).

[14]See Jon D. Levenson, *Creation and the Persistence of Evil* (Princeton, N.J.: Princeton University Press, 1988). Though it should be readily admitted that the poetic tradition will reflect on creation using language of conflict between Yahweh and the monsters of the sea (Leviathan, also known in ancient Canaanite literature as an associate of the god Yam, see Ps 74). However, here we see the poets using artistic license to make the point that Yahweh, not Baal, controls the forces of chaos. Such poetic expressions shouldn't be read as normative statements about how creation actually took place.

[15]Even further, it is likely that Genesis 1 at least implies that God created the watery mass rather than assuming that it was simply there, which seems to be the case with other creation texts. However, the issue whether Genesis 1 teaches "creation from nothing" is not a simple one. It will be discussed in chap. 7.

Chapter 5: Noah and Utnapishtim

[1]The story is recounted most recently in Karen Rhea Nemet-Nejat, *Daily Life in Mesopotamia* (Peabody, Mass.: Hendrickson, 1998), pp. 5-6.

[2]Franz Delitzsch, *Babel und Bibel* (Leipzig: Hinrichs, 1903).

[3]A point made by John H. Walton, *Ancient Israelite Literature in Its Cultural Context* (Grand Rapids: Zondervan, 1989), p. 20.

[4]We know that Gilgamesh was an actual king around which these legends grew. See Jeffrey Tigay, *The Evolution of the Gilgamesh Epic* (Philadelphia: University of Pennsylvania Press, 1982), pp. 13-16.

[5]The Gilgamesh Epic as we have it today has a final twelfth tablet, but most scholars are convinced it was added later and bears no real connection to the story told thus far.

[6]The translation here and elsewhere in this chapter of the Gilgamesh Epic is by Benjamin R. Foster and is taken from *The Context of Scripture*, ed. William W. Hallo and K. Lawson Younger Jr. (Boston: Brill, 1997), 1:460.

Chapter 6: Abraham and Nuzi

[1]A.D. is an abbreviation for *anno Domini*, which is Latin for "year of the Lord." Today we know now that when this dating system was established, there was a miscalculation of the exact year Christ was born, but this issue is not relevant to the point we are making in the chapter.

[2]See Eugene H. Merrill's article "Chronology," in *Dictionary of the Old Testament: Pentateuch*, ed. T. Desmond Alexander and David W. Baker (Downers Grove, Ill.: InterVarsity Press, 2003), p. 117.

[3]This date is debated among Bible scholars. For arguments in support of the fifteenth-

century date, see Iain Provan, V. Philips Long and Tremper Longman III, *A Biblical History of Israel* (Louisville: Westminster John Knox, 2003), pp. 131-32, and in support of a thirteenth-century date, which takes the 480 year figure as symbolic, see Kenneth A. Kitchen, *On the Reliability of the Old Testament* (Grand Rapids: Eerdmans, 2003), pp. 307-10.

[4]These and other ambiguities are presented in John Bright, *A History of Israel,* 2nd ed. (Philadelphia: Westminster Press, 1972), pp. 120-21.

[5]It's not that Nuzi has produced the only relevant material for such study. There are other important sites as well including Mari and Emar, and there are other significant Old Babylonian texts too. However, my purpose is not to be exhaustive but rather illustrative.

[6]Barry L. Eichler, "Nuzi and the Bible: A Retrospective," in *DUMU-E$_2$-DUB-BA-A: Studies in Honor of Ake W. Sjöberg,* ed. H. Behrens et al. (Philadelphia: Samuel Noah Kramer Fund, 1989), 108-9.

[7]The scholars who argued this way from the 1930s through the early 1960s include some of the most influential of the period: William F. Albright, Cyrus Gordon, E. A. Speiser and John Bright.

[8]Here I will be describing the position of E. A. Speiser as found in *Genesis,* Anchor Bible (Garden Grove, N.Y.: Doubleday, 1964), and "The Wife-Sister Motif in the Patriarchal Narratives," in *Oriental and Biblical Studies,* ed. J. J. Finkelstein and M. Greenburg (Philadelphia: University of Pennsylvania Press, 1967), pp. 62-82.

[9]John Bright, *A History of Israel,* 2nd ed. (Philadelphia: Westminster Press, 1972), p. 79.

[10]See Thomas L. Thompson, *The Historicity of the Patriarchal Narratives,* Beihefte zur Zeitschrift für die alttestamentliche Wissenschaft 133 (Berlin: De Gruyter 1974); John Van Seters, *Abraham in History and Tradition* (New Haven, Conn.: Yale University Press, 1975).

[11]For detailed studies of these, see Martin J. Selman, "Comparative Customs and the Patriarchal Age," in *Essays in the Patriarchal Narratives,* ed. A. R. Millard and D. J. Wiseman (Leicester, U.K.: Inter-Varsity Press, 1980), pp. 91-140; Eichler, "Nuzi and the Bible," pp. 107-19.

[12]See the discussion by E. A. Speiser, "Notes to Recently Published Nuzi Texts," *Journal of the American Oriental Society* 55 (1935): 435-36, and Cyrus H. Gordon, "Biblical Customs and the Nuzu Tablets," *Biblical Archaeologist* 3 (1940): 2-3.

[13]I am indebted to the discussion found in Victor P. Hamilton, *The Book of Genesis 1—17* (Grand Rapids: Eerdmans, 1990), pp. 430-34.

[14]D. J. Wiseman, "Abban and Alalah," *Journal of Cuneiform Studies* 12 (1958): 129.

[15]O. Gurney, *The Hittites* (Baltimore: Penguin, 1954), p. 151.

[16]Gordon, "Biblical Customs and the Nuzu Tablets," p. 3.

[17]However as Hamilton also points out, this custom can't be used to date Abraham to the second millennium since the occurrence of this custom also in the first century shows that it was a long-lived institution.

Part IV: Reading Genesis as God's Story

[1]C. Marvin Pate et al., *The Story of Israel: A Biblical Theology* (Downers Grove, Ill.: Inter-Varsity Press, 2004), p. 30. This book and Gordon J. Wenham's *Story as Torah: Reading the Bible Ethically* (Grand Rapids: Baker, 2004) have been particularly helpful in shaping my thinking about the theological coherence of Genesis.

Chapter 7: The Primeval History

[1]See the discussion by C. John Collins, *Science and Faith: Friends or Foes?* (Wheaton, Ill.: Crossway, 2003), pp. 66-68.

[2]Walter Brueggemann, *Genesis* (Atlanta: John Knox Press, 1982), pp. 31-2.

[3]For further reading on the relationship between science and the biblical account of creation, see C. John Collins, *Science and Faith: Friends or Foes?* (Wheaton, Ill.: Crossway, 2003), plus the texts he cites.

[4]Dan B. Allender and Tremper Longman III, *Intimate Allies* (Wheaton, Ill.: Tyndale House, 1995) explores the implications of Genesis 1—3 for our present understanding of marriage. Regarding sabbath observance, see Tremper Longman III, *Immanuel in Our Place: Seeing Christ in Israel's Worship* (Phillipsburg, N.J.: Presbyterian & Reformed, 2001), pp. 163-84.

[5]The argument is that it is like the so-called Sumerian Dispute texts like "The Debate Between Ewe and Wheat," "Hoe and Plow," "Bird and Fish" and "Summer and Winter" (see *The Context of Scripture,* ed. William W. Hallo and K. Lawson Younger Jr. [Boston: Brill, 1997], 1:575-87).

[6]This is in the original edition of the NLT. The revision published in 2004 has gone to a more traditional and literal translation.

[7]J. P. Fokkelman, *Narrative Art in Genesis* (Amsterdam: Van Gorcum, 1975).

[8]Robert R. Wilson, *Genealogy and History in the Biblical World* (New Haven, Conn.: Yale University Press, 1977).

[9]So C. John Collins, *Science and Faith: Friends or Foes?* (Wheaton: Crossway, 2003), pp. 107-9.

Chapter 8: The Patriarchal Narratives

[1]Gordon J. Wenham, *Story as Torah: Reading Old Testament Narrative Ethically* (Grand Rapids: Baker, 2004), p. 37.

[2]Though it is only later that the patriarch had his name changed from Abram to Abraham, I will refer to him by the better known, longer version throughout. I will explain the significance of the name change at the appropriate point in the story. The same approach will be taken to Sarah, who early in the narrative goes by the name Sarai.

[3]The idea that the patriarchal narratives, in particular the Abraham narrative, should be understood as the story of the patriarch's response to threats and obstacles to the fulfillment of the divine promises was most clearly argued by D. J. A. Clines, *The Theme of the Pentateuch,* 2nd ed. (Sheffield, U.K.: JSOT Press, 2002).

[4]We noted a similar practice with the rainbow at the time of Noah.

[5]See Gen 25:19-26; 30:22-24; Judg 13; 1 Sam 1 respectively.

[6]For the meaning and function of *toledot,* see chap. 3 (p. 60).

[7]Robert Alter, *The Art of Biblical Narrative* (New York: Basic Books, 1981), p. 180. Alter calls this "narrative analogy."

[8]Victor Hamilton, *The Book of Genesis: Chapters 1-15,* New International Commentary: Old Testament (Grand Rapids: Eerdmans, 1995), pp. 294-95.

Chapter 9: The Joseph Story

[1]See Tremper Longman III, *Immanuel in Our Place* (Phillipsburg, N.J.: Presbyterian & Reformed, 2001), pp. 122-24.

Chapter 10: The Christological Difference

[1]For a fuller account of these chapters, see pp. 101-14. This brief summary is placed here for the convenience of the reader.

[2]Consult any modern commentary on these chapters.

[3]See for instance, Gordon Wenham, *Genesis 1—15,* Word Biblical Commentary (Waco, Tex.: Word, 1987), p. 80.

[4]This position understands *uru* as an ancient determinative indicating a city name.

[5]Especially in the light of the fact that Jewish literature in the period just before Jesus understood Psalm 110 messianically (Dead Sea Scrolls [the Genesis Apocryphon, 1QapGen, and the Melchizedek scroll, 11QMelch]) as well as Jesus' interaction with Jewish leaders in Mt 22:41-45).

Names Index

Aalders, G. Charles, 177
Albright, William F., Jr., 185
Alexander, T. Desmond, 56, 57, 182
Allender, Dan, 186
Allis, Oswald T., 182
Alter, Robert, 54, 67, 181, 182, 183, 186
Arnold, Bill T., 98
Beckwith, Roger T., 182
Berlin, Adele, 67
Blomberg, Craig L., 39
Bloom, Harold, 57, 182
Borgman, Paul, 183
Breyer, Bryan E., 98
Bright, John, 93, 185
Brueggemann, Walter, 177, 182, 183, 186
Carr, David M., 57
Cassuto, Umberto, 57, 177, 182
Chavalas, Mark W., 98
Clifford, Richard J., 98
Clines, D. J. A., 186
Coats, George W., 183
Collins, C. John, 185, 186
Currid, John D., 183
Dalley, Stephanie, 98
Delitzsch, Franz, 81
Delitzsch. Frederick, 81, 184
Dijk, Jacobus van, 183

Eichler, Barry L., 92, 98, 185
Eissfeldt, Otto, 182
Fee, Gordon D., 39, 181
Fokkelman, J. P., 67, 183, 186
Foster, Benjamin R., 183, 184
Fredricks, Cathi J., 178
Garrett, Duane, 57
Goldingay, John, 182
Gordon, Cyrus, 185
Gunkel, Hermann, 183
Gurney, O., 185
Hallo, William W., 98, 183, 184, 186
Hamilton, Victor P., 97, 178, 185, 186
Hartley, John E., 178
Heidel, Alexander, 98
Howard, David M., 183
Hubbard, Robert L., 39
Jacobsen, Thorkild, 184
Kikawada, Isaac M., 54, 58, 182
Kitchen, Kenneth A., 54, 58, 182, 185
Klein, William W., 39
Kramer, Samuel N., 184
Lambert, W. G., 98, 183
Leech, G. N., 182
Levenson, Jon D., 98, 184
Long, V. Phillips, 62-63, 182, 183, 185
Longman, Tremper, III, 39, 67, 181, 182, 183, 185, 186
Matthews, Victor H., 98
McConville, J. Gordon, 182
Merrill, Eugene H., 184
Michie, Donald, 65, 183
Millard, A. R., 98, 183

Moberley, Walter, 183
Nemet-Nejat, Karen Rhea, 184
Pate, C. Marvin, 185
Pritchard, James B., 98
Provan, Iain, 182, 183, 185
Quinn, Arthur, 54, 58, 182
Ridderbos, Herman, 181
Rhoads, David, 65, 183
Ross, Allen P., 178
Rosenberg, David, 57, 182
Sailhamer, John H., 183
Sarna, Nahum M., 178
Selman, Martin J., 98, 185
Short, M. H., 182
Silva, Moisés, 39
Soggin, J. Alberto, 182
Speiser, E. A., 182, 185
Sternberg, Meir, 67
Stuart, Douglas, 39, 181
Thompson, Thomas L., 94, 185
Tigay, Jeffrey, 98, 184
Van Seters, John, 61, 182, 185
Vanhoozer, Kevin J., 39
Wallace, Howard N., 184
Waltke, Bruce K., 66, 178, 183
Walton, John H., 98, 179, 181, 184
Wellhausen, Julius, 55
Wenham, Gordon J., 39, 54, 58, 179, 182, 185, 186, 187
Whybray, R. Norman, 54, 58, 182
Wilson, Robert R., 186
Wiseman, D. J., 185
Young, Edward J., 182
Younger, K. Lawson, Jr., 98, 183, 184, 186

Subject Index

Abraham, 14, 20, 27, 30, 36, 45-46, 57, 58, 61-62, 64, 66, 72, 88, 90-97, 100-101, 125-39, 141, 143, 147-51, 160, 166, 169-74

Adam and Eve, 15, 36, 47, 51, 63, 69, 77-78, 81, 87, 101-2, 105-6, 108-15, 123, 125, 128, 166, 169

Atrahasis, 75, 77, 80, 82, 106

Babel, 64, 114, 119, 125

blessing, 14-15, 100, 102, 114, 125-30, 133-34, 136, 138, 142, 148, 150, 153, 159, 160-61, 171, 173

Cain, 36, 66, 112-15, 123-24

chronology, 52, 89, 90, 127

circumcision, 36, 133, 146

covenant, 29-30, 35-36, 66, 95-96, 118-19, 127, 132-33, 139, 141, 146-47, 160, 170, 173-74

creation, 13, 15, 17, 22, 24-26, 28, 31, 34-36, 46, 48, 51, 53, 60, 64, 69-79, 82, 84, 88, 97, 100-110, 117-18, 126-27, 166

documentary hypothesis, 46, 49-56, 91-92, 96

Egyptian literature, 25, 27, 71, 73-74, 77, 79, 130, 132, 153, 156-58

Enuma Elish, 22, 25, 71, 74-77, 79, 106

ethics, 135

Fall, 103, 108-14, 121

flood, 17, 20, 24, 53, 69, 70-71, 81-88, 97, 101, 114, 116-17, 119

Garden of Eden, 15, 29, 48, 51, 80, 100-101, 106, 108, 112, 114-15, 125, 128, 166

genealogy, 13, 52, 60, 116, 121-25, 167

Genesis
authorship, 18, 21-22, 26, 29-31, 33, 43-45, 47, 49, 53-56, 59-63, 65, 72, 78, 80, 100, 116-18, 163-69, 172-75

title, 14, 32

genre, 23, 26, 59-61, 65, 67, 123

Gilgamesh Epic, 81-87, 98

history, 13-16, 23-28, 31, 33, 35, 45, 49, 55, 57, 60-66, 71-73, 89-92, 112, 122, 134, 140, 161, 164, 173, 175

image of God, 28, 36, 78, 105, 118

Isaac, 47, 54, 58, 63-64, 91, 100, 125, 127, 134-36, 138-40, 144, 147-49

Jacob, 36, 47, 63-64, 90-91, 100, 125, 127, 136-51, 156-60, 174

Joseph, 14, 20, 24, 26-27, 36, 46, 48, 50-51, 62, 64, 90, 99, 100, 127, 140, 144, 147-51, 153-60, 166, 174

Mari, 27, 96, 131

marriage, 92-93, 108-9, 140-41, 145-46, 151

Melchizedek, 20, 166, 170-74

metaphor, 15, 29-30, 73, 103

minimalism, 26

myth, 23, 26, 42, 60-61, 71, 73-74, 77, 79, 86, 110, 122

narrative, 36, 41, 50, 52-54, 60-61, 63, 65-66, 76, 93, 100, 106, 109, 111, 122, 124-26, 128-29, 131, 134, 136-38, 140, 144-47, 153, 155-56, 160, 166-67, 171-72, 174

Nephilim, 20, 116

Nuzi, 27, 91-98, 131, 142

promises, 21, 64, 66, 95-96, 100, 116, 119, 126, 128-37, 139, 141, 146-47, 150, 152, 159-60, 166, 169, 170-71

sabbath, 108-9

source criticism, 14, 24, 41, 46-57, 65, 102, 104

structure, 23, 30, 47, 59-65, 67, 109, 118, 120

style, literary, 54, 64-65, 67, 99

Ugaritic literature, 21, 25, 71, 76

Ur, 27, 45, 127-29, 132

work, 15, 37-38, 56, 76, 80, 103, 106, 108-9, 113-15, 118, 140, 169

Scripture Index

Genesis

1, *20, 28, 48, 52, 77, 103,*
117, 127, 184
1—2, *15, 72, 77, 79, 100,*
102-9, 118, 126, 128
1—11, *64, 99, 101, 102-25,*
126
1:1, *64*
1:1—2:3, *47, 51*
1:1—2:4, *24, 48, 102*
1:1—11:26, *64*
1:4, *107*
1:6, *77*
1:12, *107*
1:18, *107*
1:21, *107*
1:25, *107*
1:26-27, *28, 105, 118*
1:27, *108, 121*
1:28-31, *106*
1:28, *15, 84, 118*
1:31, *107*
2:1-3, *109*
2:4, *47, 63, 102*
2:4-25, *24, 51*
2:5, *48*
2:7, *106*
2:15, *106, 109, 114*
2:15-17, *118*
2:17, *112*
2:18, *108*
2:18-25, *109*

2:20, *106*
2:21, *106*
2:24, *109*
3—11, *15, 29, 79, 100,*
113, 126
3:1, *167*
3:3, *110*
3:5, *111*
3:6, *111*
3:10, *112*
3:11-13, *112*
3:15, *112, 123, 125,*
166-69
3:16, *113*
3:17-19, *109, 114*
3:22-24, *114*
4, *66, 115, 116*
4—11, *112*
4:4, *115*
4:7, *113*
4:11-12, *115*
4:17-26, *112, 167*
4:17—5:32, *122, 123-25*
5, *60, 113, 116, 122, 123,*
167
5:1, *63*
6—9, *84*
6:1-6, *116-17*
6:4, *116*
6:5, *84, 117*
6:6, *117*
6:7, *117*
6:9, *63, 84, 118*
6:11-12, *117*
6:13-21, *117*
7, *118*
8—9, *118*
8:1, *118*
8:6-12, *85*
8:21, *118*
8:22, *119*
9, *30, 118*
9:1, *118*

9:2-3, *118*
9:11, *119*
10, *119, 121, 122, 123,*
125
10:1, *47, 63*
11, *100*
11:1-9, *119, 120*
11:10, *47, 63*
11:27—50:26, *64*
11:27, *63, 125, 126*
11:28, *45*
11:31, *45*
12, *101, 136*
12—26, *171*
12—36, *64, 100, 126-48*
12—50, *100*
12:1, *64, 127*
12:1-3, *66, 132, 169-70*
12:2-3, *128*
12:4-5, *90*
12:6-9, *129*
12:10-20, *24, 50, 54, 93*
13, *130, 172*
14, *27, 35, 45, 60, 131, 171,*
172
14:14, *46*
14:17-20, *170-74*
15, *30, 51, 95, 96*
15—17, *131*
15:1, *131*
15:2-3, *95*
15:2, *169*
15:7, *45*
15:9, *95*
15:17, *132*
16, *132*
17, *30, 132*
18, *133*
18:10, *133*
18:12, *133*
18:14, *133*
18:16—19:38, *133*
20, *50, 130, 134, 136*

20:1-18, *24, 93*
20:1-17, *54*
21, *134*
21:6-7, *134*
21:12, *136*
22:1, *134*
22:2, *135*
24, *37*
25, *147*
25:11, *136*
25:19, *136*
25:12, *63*
25:19, *47, 63*
25:19-26, *186*
25:23, *137, 138*
26, *50*
26:1-25, *54*
26:1-11, *24*
26:24, *136*
26:35, *138*
27, *138*
27:41-46, *142*
28:3-4, *139*
28:13-15, *139*
29:14, *140*
29:31, *140*
30:22-24, *186*
30:39, *141*
31:3, *142*
31:9, *141*
31:33-34, *93*
32, *143*
32:1-2, *142*
32:32, *143*
34, *145, 157*
34:3, *145*
34:5, *145*
34:30, *146*
35:3, *147*
35:11-13, *147*
35:18, *147*
35:22, *159*
35:27-29, *147*

36, *147*
36:1, *47, 63*
36:9, *47, 63*
37, *48, 55, 64, 150*
37—50, *64, 100, 149-61*
37:2, *47, 63, 149*
37:5-11, *50*
37:12-36, *182*
37:25-28, *48*
37:28, *24, 50*
37:36, *153*
38, *149, 151-53*
38:9, *153*
39, *153*
39—50, *64*
39:2-3, *153*
39:6, *153*
39:8-9, *153*
39:23, *154*
40:8, *154*
40:14-15, *155*
40:23, *155*
41, *155*
41:16, *155*
45:5, *158*
45:7-8, *158*
48, *159*
49, *28, 60, 159, 161*
49:5-7, *157*
50:19-20, *150*
50:20, *174*
50:25, *161*

Exodus
2:15-17, *140*
12:40, *90*
17:14, *44*
19—24, *35*
20, *55, 56, 182*
20:7, *111*
20:8-11, *109*
20:24-26, *50*
24:4, *44*

25—40, *50*
32—34, *160*
34:27, *44*

Leviticus
1—9, *50*

Numbers
32, *51*
33:2, *44*

Deuteronomy
12, *52, 56, 182*
12:10, *56*
18:10, *154*
25:5-10, *152*
31:22, *44*
32, *44*
33:29, *108*
34, *45*

Joshua
1, *44*
1:6-7, *44*
24:2, *129*

Judges
13, *186*
17—18, *46*

1 Samuel
1, *186*

2 Samuel
7, *160, 173, 174*
7:1, *56*

1 Kings
6:1, *88, 90*
13, *139*

2 Kings
22—23, *52*

2 Chronicles
25:4, *45*

Ezra
6:18, *45*

Nehemiah
1:11, *154*
13:1, *45*

Psalms
2, *173*
14:1, *107*
29:1, *116*
33:20, *108*
53:1, *107*
74, *184*
78:65, *29*
89:18-19, *108*
104:15, *111*
110, *173, 174, 187*
131, *108*

Proverbs
1:7, *107*
1:20-32, *108*
5—7, *153*
8—9, *108*

Song of Songs
7:10, *113*

Isaiah
14, *110, 167*
66:13, *108*

Jeremiah
31:33-35, *19*

Ezekiel
28, *167*

Daniel
2, *154*

Matthew
1:1, *174*
9:27, *174*
12:23, *174*
19:7, *45*
22:24, *45*
22:41-45, *187*
22:43, *174*
22:45, *174*

Mark
7:10, *45*
12:26, *45*

Luke
20:27-40, *117*
24, *164, 165*
24:22-27, *163*
24:25-27, *32*
24:44-49, *32*
24:44-48, *163*

John
1:17, *45*
5:46, *45*
7:23, *45*

Acts
2:22-24, *174-75*

Romans
1:3, *174*

16:20, *110*

1 Corinthians
1:28, *18*

Galatians
3:15-16, *169-70*
3:29, *170*

Colossians
2:15, *113*

2 Timothy
2:8, *174*

Hebrews
2:14-15, *168*
4:14—5:10, *170*
5:9-20, *171*
7:1-9:13, *170*
7:10, *173*
11:3, *103*
11:17-19, *135*

1 Peter
1:10-12, *182*
2:9, *19*

Jude
6, *116*

Revelation
4:11, *103*
12:7-9, *168*
12:9, *110*
20, *15*
20:7-10, *169*
21—22, *15*

DATE DUE

DATE DUE